# THE COMPLETE ILLUSTRATED
# BOOK OF DYES
# FROM NATURAL SOURCES

# THE COMPLETE ILLUSTRATED
# BOOK OF DYES
# FROM NATURAL SOURCES

Arnold and Connie Krochmal

Doubleday & Company, Inc., Garden City, New York
1974

Library of Congress Cataloging in Publication Data

Krochmal, Arnold, 1919–
 The complete illustrated book of dyes from natural sources.

 Bibliography: p. 257
 1. Dyes and dyeing.  2. Dye plants.  I. Krochmal, Connie, joint author.
II. Title.
TP919.K76    646.6′3
ISBN 0-385-05653-2 Trade
      0-385-05656-7 Paper
Library of Congress Catalog Card Number 73–9167

We dedicate this book to our dear and loved friend
Morton J. Green, M.D.,
childhood companion and lifelong friend, whose
compassion and concern have been a staff to lean on
when the path was arduous.

ARNOLD AND CONNIE KROCHMAL
*Raleigh, North Carolina*

## ACKNOWLEDGMENTS

We are deeply grateful to a number of people who assisted us during the writing of this book.

Dr. Earl Core, University of West Virginia, and Rita Adrosko, Curator, Textile Division, Smithsonian Institution, provided generously of a range of photos and illustrations we wanted.

Don Dedera, a kindred spirit, not only lent us some of his color work, but dug up some useful and hard-to-find information about Indian dyes in Arizona. Troy Gruber, Bureau of Indian Affairs, Washington, D.C., was of tremendous help in locating outstanding photos of Indians and their weaving and dyeing activities.

Dr. Edward Ross, California Academy of Sciences; Dr. Carl E. Anderson, School of Medicine, University of North Carolina; Dr. James B. Pritchard, University of Pennsylvania Museum, and Dr. G. W. Dekkle, Florida State Department of Agriculture, all provided unusual and interesting photos.

Lucia H. Jaycocks, Historic Sites Coordinator, Charles Towne Landing, Charleston, South Carolina, let us use her file on indigo and provided information as well as the pleasure of seeing the indigo garden. Martha LaFrance, FAO Rome, was kind in sending village scenes. The Information Division, Military Governor's Office, Kano, Nigeria, went to great trouble to take and send photos of the fascinating Kano dye pits. Karl Graetz, Soil Conservation Service, U.S.D.A., Raleigh, N.C., was most helpful.

The Charleston Library Society and the libraries of the University of North Carolina and the Duke University School of Medicine permitted us to use illustrations from some of their rare and old books. The Penland School of Crafts and the Great Smoky Mountains National Park provided photos.

As always, our friend Dr. Isaac Littleton, Director of the D. H.

ACKNOWLEDGMENTS

Hill Library, North Carolina State University, Raleigh, N.C., and his enthusiastic staff provided all of the assistance and help we asked for.

Ms. Mary Cowell, Photo Librarian, Information Division, United States Department of Agriculture, was most helpful in helping locate certain photos.

Professor Glenn W. Toomey and Dr. John C. Rice, Department of Crops Science, North Carolina State University, Raleigh, provided photos of cotton and tobacco.

# Contents

1.  Drying wool in the village of Varamch, Iran. As part of rural development in Iran a wool rug dyeing and weaving industry is being established with help from the FAO/Freedom from Hunger Campaign. (*Food and Agriculture Organization, United Nations, Rome*)

# Introduction

All over the world there is a growing interest and enthusiasm for the skills and crafts of our parents. Weaving, spinning, and dyeing are in the forefront of this return to the use of our own hands and talents.

The Food and Agriculture Organization and Freedom from Hunger Fund have sponsored programs which encourage the revival of traditional crafts and skills in Iran (Figure 1) and Burma (Figure 2), to name only two. In Guatemala a high level of craft skills in the weaving and dyeing of cotton has created an international reputation for rugs, shirts, and serapes, all based on hand skills.

When Arnold lived in Afghanistan, many interesting hours were

2. Block printing as a village craft industry, using locally woven fabrics and natural dyes, is a source of income in Burma. (*Food and Agriculture Organization, United Nations, Rome*)

spent in the rug factories, often centered in poor houses, in western Afghanistan at Herat. Driving from Greece to Jerusalem, he saw in every large village a small dye work, and most of the village women still spinning yarns and dyeing them. Some of the village weavings he brought from Greece have been given to the School of Textiles of North Carolina State University, Raleigh.

The reviving and growing interest in the United States is well recognized. The Great Smoky Mountains National Park, straddling the North Carolina-Tennessee border, sponsors a summer demonstration of spinning, weaving, and dyeing. In our home state of North Carolina one of the nation's outstanding crafts schools, Penland School of Handicrafts, Penland, offers outstanding programs in the use of natural dyes.

In writing this book we have combined our individual expertise. Connie, from southeastern Kentucky, a part of Appalachia famous for its use of plants for a wide range of home uses, has brought her practical knowledge and experience. Arnold, an economic botanist, has added his knowledge and love of plants, as well as the experience gained living in odd corners of the world.

One of the most fascinating aspects of natural dyes is the variability and unpredictability of the colors one can expect, even under what appears to be uniform conditions. The plants themselves vary, depending on their age, soil conditions, and growing conditions; the dyer will vary in the techniques used as to timing, mordanting, dyeing, and subsequent procedures. The basic materials dyed will differ as well. All of this, we feel, adds to the pleasure and spice of using natural dyes and provides a charming variability not approached by synthetic dyes. The warmth of natural colors has a glow, the glow of nature and man working in close conjunction. To us even a less than ideal color has a warmth and beauty to it, when we think of the plant and the circumstances under which the plant grew.

We strongly urge that you buy your plant materials from available sources, some of which we have listed, as a precautionary measure to protect certain wild plants from depletion.

A lumber mill is a fine source of barks and some woods. Health food stores and organic food stores can provide a surprising number of roots, leaves, and flowers useful in dyeing, usually in the form of dried plants packaged and marketed as teas.

In harvesting plant materials remember that fruits and nuts can be harvested freely without fear of destroying the plant populations. Roots and barks are another matter, and can, if carried to extremes, jeopardize plant communities. Bloodroot, yellowroot, goldenroot, and other plants whose roots have been in demand in the past are in precarious positions today.

Common weeds, such as goldenrod, pokeweed, docks, and plantains, and garden plants can be harvested freely without fear of depletion. However, recent reports from England note the rapid disappearance of dandelion from suburban areas.

# CHAPTER 1

# In the Beginning

*"And Mordecai went out from the presence of the king in royal apparel of blue and white, and with a great crown of gold and with a garment of fine linen, and purple . . ."*   ESTHER 8:15

*"Thou shalt make the tabernacle with ten curtains of fine twisted linen, and blue and purple and scarlet . . ."*   EXODUS 26:1

Color has always fascinated man, and from his earliest time he has tried to duplicate the colors of nature. Color has been, and is, interwoven in the fabric of our lives. We wear black to symbolize mourning; Chinese wear white. Purple at one time was the color of royalty.

From earliest times men have used natural dyes to ornament their bodies, their caves, and their wearing apparel, in bright colors, mostly derived from plants, but in a few cases from insects, animals, and sea creatures.

In Egypt of the Pharaohs fabrics were woven (Figure 3) from linen, dyed, and used to clothe the living and wrap the dead. The Greeks and Romans wove wool and linen, imported dyes, and made their clothing and bedclothes (Figure 4). The flourishing Indian, Chinese, and Japanese civilizations used natural dyes extensively, as did the Aztecs, Incas, Mayas, and Indians of the New World.

## Major Plant Dyes

Three dye plants have been of major commercial importance in the history of dyeing. These were indigo, madder, and woad.

3. Weaving and dyeing were basic occupations in ancient Egypt. The model of a weaving shop, dating from about 2000 B.C., was found in an Egyptian tomb. (*Metropolitan Museum of Art, Anonymous Gift, 1930*)

A multitude of other plants have done yeoman service, in peace as well as war. The butternut color of the Confederate Army uniforms was from the nut of *Juglans cinerea*. Settlers busily dyed the yarns and fibers they spun in the yard or barn (Figure 5), using recipes passed down from mother to daughter (Figure 6).

As early as the Revolution dye mills were to be found in New York,

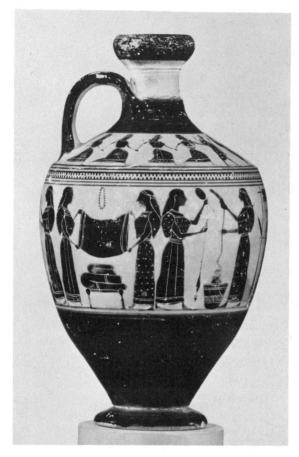

4. An ancient Greek vase from about 560 B.C., showing women working wool on a loom. (*Metropolitan Museum of Art, Fletcher Fund, 1931*)

Boston, and Philadelphia (Figure 7), meeting city dwellers' needs for clothing and fabrics. As the nineteenth century came to a close, less and less home dyeing was done, and more and more factory-dyed materials found their way into rural homes.

## INDIGO

Perhaps of greatest interest is indigo because of its long history, going back to Sanskrit records four thousand years old, and its period of success in South Carolina. A number of plants have been called indigo, some related to the "real" plant, *Indigofera tinctoria*, and others only resembling it.

5. An old dyeing arrangement in North Carolina. Large copper pots were used in a brick stove fed with wood. (*Penland School of Handicrafts, Penland, N.C.*)

The indigo plant is a shrubby legume, growing to five feet in height, with dainty compound leaves and typical legume pods.*

Indigos were cultivated, as well as harvested wild, in India (Figure 8), Egypt, and by the Incas of Peru. Remains of ancient fabrics recovered from tombs strongly indicate an indigo color in use for scores of centuries.

As European explorers began to carry their new-found knowledge and wealth to Europe, indigo was reintroduced to the world market. In the twelfth century Jewish refugees from Iraq, an indigo center, were responsible for the large scale use of indigo in the local

* Live plants may be seen growing at Charles Towne Landing, Charleston, South Carolina, once the capital of the American indigo trade.

Red on Cotton & Wool
100 lbs Cloth = 2½ Pails of Sumac
in Cold water pass it over the
reail 5 or 6 times then let it down
in liquor & lay 10 or 12 hours
then take it out & give a Slight
wash = then in a hot tub use
25 lbs Alum = 6 lbs Argol 1 lb
Blue vitriol — Cool down a little
enter pieces & boil 1½ hours
take out Cool well — fold up
and Cover so the outer folds will
not dry let them lay 2 days
then give another Slight wash
        Then in fresh water use
75 lbs Peachwood Boil 1½ hours
Cool down well — add 1 pink
Muriate of Tin — take up
enter cloth run ¼ hour without
Steam then raise gradualy to a
Boil & Boil to required Shade
        A good quality of Hyperic
will answer if Peachwood
can not be had

6. This hand-written dye recipe book from the early 1800s uses sumac berries for a red dye for cotton or wool. (*Krochmal Collection, D. H. Hill Library, North Carolina State University*)

7. This is the earliest recorded illustration of an American dye factory, about 1836. At the left a worker is lifting a bucket of dye from a vat heated by a furnace. The clothes hanging from the ceiling are part of a piece-dying process. (*Smithsonian Institution, Division of Textiles, Rita Adrosko*)

8. A sketch of indigo dyeing in India during the 1600s by a French visitor. The sketch shows workers cutting the plants in the background, placing the stalks in water-filled vats, agitating the soaking indigo stalks, and carrying the precipitated dye material to dry. (*Smithsonian Institution, Division of Textiles, Rita Adrosko*)

textile works in Venice, where increased skill in its use resulted in increased employment of the dye.

In the late 1500s and early 1600s the popularity of indigo caused it to be banned in England, the German states, and France because growers of woad in these countries fought to continue to monopolize the market. Gradually the restrictive laws were lifted and indigo replaced woad in the 1700s.

The indigo industry in Charleston, South Carolina, in the 1700s was the indirect result of England capturing Jamaica, with its indigo plantations, from Spain. The policy of Parliament in 1660 to increase sugar production in Jamaica by means of a tax on Jamaican indigo coming into the British Isles ended indigo production in Jamaica.

At that time planters in Charleston were experimenting with a wide variety of crops, including rice, tea, sugar, pomegranates, and indigo.

9.   An issue of *Gentlemen's Magazine,* published in London in 1755, provided this working sketch of machinery used in the indigo trade in the colonies. The caption read: "Representation of the Machine Used in Making Indigo; (a) two pumps in a frame worked by a pendulum to pump water into the steeper (b); (c) the beater; (d) a vat of lime-water; (e) a tub set to receive the muddy water from the beater; (f) a stage whereon to work the pumps. All this except the pumps is necessary for every 6 to 7 acres you plant." (*University of North Carolina Library, Chapel Hill, N.C.*)

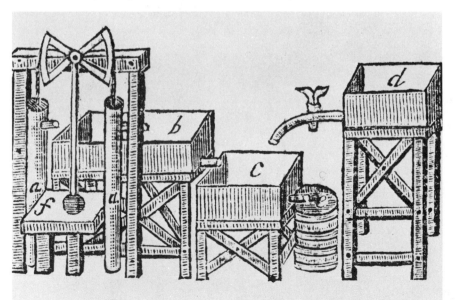

Eliza Lucas Pinckney is credited as the person who really founded a successful indigo industry in South Carolina. With seeds her father, the Governor of Antigua, sent her, she experimented until she was able to successfully grow enough indigo to ship to England in 1747.

The need for food during the Revolution caused rice to replace indigo in the Charleston countryside, and when the war ended, competition from India ended commercial indigo in South Carolina. Cotton moved in, never to be usurped.

The basic method used to extract indigo is a simple one (Figure 9). When the plants are about to bloom, they are harvested, placed in large tanks of water, and allowed to ferment. After a week or so the liquid is drawn off, the plant residues are stirred to mix in air and allowed to set for a period of time. When the solution has settled, the clear top water is drawn off and the remaining residue reduced in volume by sun drying or heating over a fire. The solid matter then

10.   One of the few places in the world where indigo dyeing is still carried on is in Kano, Nigeria. This photo shows the pits in use. (*Military Governor's Office, Information Division, Kano State, Nigeria*)

is dried and made into balls. It is estimated that sixty to seventy pounds of fresh plants are required to make one to two pounds of indigo dye.

Indigo dye is insoluble in water. To use it as a dye and to aid its absorption into fabrics, a two-step procedure, given in the chapter on blue dyes, is necessary.

We know of two places in the world today where indigo is still in general use, in Kano State, Nigeria (Figure 10), and in Guatemala. Other areas may exist, and we would welcome information about them from readers of the book.

## WOAD

"Why is blue specified for the holy fringes? Because it is the color of sea and sky, suggestive of the sapphire of the Throne of Glory." (The *Talmud*, referring to the prayer shawl used in synagogues.)

Woad, *Isatis tinctoria,* is thought to have been known in the Holy Land in biblical times and may have been used to dye the robes of the high priests in Jerusalem. We believe that the blue corners of the prayer shawls were dyed with woad.

Julius Caesar commented on its use in England and Gaul. The Celts of Roman times were noted for painting themselves blue with woad, to throw fear into their enemies. Pliny the Elder reported Gallic women painted their bodies with woad for certain ceremonies.

The plant was cultivated extensively all over Europe and was the major dye used until the late 1600s and early 1700s, when it was replaced by the better indigo dyes.

Some efforts were made to grow woad in the United States, particularly in Connecticut, in colonial times. The high labor requirements for processing the plants ended the efforts.

The plants, which are distantly related to cabbages, grow to four feet in height and have yellow flowers (Figure 11).

The dye is made from the leaves, which are chopped or ground and then placed in small piles to dry. When the piles are semidry, they are packed into balls about the size of a softball.

The balls are allowed to dry in a shaded, well-ventilated area for four to six weeks, and are then ground to powder, spread three to four inches deep in a shaded area, dampened, and turned frequently. The process of wetting and turning is carried on for eight to ten weeks to allow for fermentation.

At the end of this period the sticky material is packed into wooden shipping boxes.

11. From the lovely old *Fuch's Herbal* comes this clear and accurate drawing of a woad plant in bloom. (*Duke Medical School Library*)

## MADDER

Another very old dye plant is madder, a red dye from *Rubia tinctorium* and related species. Linen dyed with madder has been found in Egyptian tombs on mummies.

Greek and Roman writers described the madder plant in detail, leaving no doubt that they were talking about *Rubia*.

For several hundred years after the fall of the Roman Empire in the fifth century, madder was of no commercial importance in Europe and was imported from the Near East. About the seventh century it began to reappear gradually in Europe as a crop.

From the early 1500s on, the Dutch were the major source of madder, followed by the French. England produced some but not much.

Madder was used to dye the famous British Army redcoat uniforms, as well as the red jackets of fox hunters. Also known as Turkey red, it was a basic and widely used dye in England and the United States in the 1700s.

The washed, fresh roots are beaten into a paste for twelve hours and are used in this form. For commercial use the roots are dried, ground to a powder, and aged in casks for one to two years. Only the roots of plants two years or older are used.

In the nineteenth century madder died out, to be replaced by the much cheaper synthetics, the fate of most natural dyes.

## *Unusual Dye Sources*

### PURPLE FROM THE SEA

The ancient Phoenician city of Tyre gave early civilization the color that came to be known as Tyrian purple. The source was a small sea snail (Figure 12), about one and one half inches long, that had to be cracked open and the tiny dye sac removed. The amount obtained from each snail was so small as to require tremendous numbers of snails and great amounts of labor.

Tyrian purple was reserved for the rulers of church and state, because the cost was very high and only the rich could afford to have materials dyed purple. Thus the phrase "born to the purple."

Related mollusks have been used in the British Isles and are used in Guatemala.

12. This is the source of Tyrian purple, a sea shell called *Murex*. (*Arnold Krochmal*)

13. A close-up of the cottony cochineal scale on a prickly-pear leaf in Florida. (*Florida Department of Agriculture and Consumer Services, Division of Plant Industry, Gainesville, Florida*)

## DYES FROM INSECTS

*". . . though thou clothest thyself with crimson . . ."*
JEREMIAH 4:30

*"And the priest shall take cedar-wood, hyssop, and scarlet, and cast it into the midst of the burning of the heifer."* NUMBERS 19:6

### COCHINEAL

In one of those marvelous facts of history that may be hard to grasp, two distinct civilizations (separated as far as we know by unexplored oceans, unpassed mountains, and uncharted seas) used the same source of crimson dye, small scale insects, called cochineal

14. The Incas of pre-Columbian times used a number of wild plants as dye sources for wearing apparel as well as decorating, in addition to the cochineal scale. This painted textile of Chima, Peru, dates from the period A.D. 1100–1400. (*Museum of Primitive Art, New York*)

in the New World, and kermes in the Old World. The cochineal is *Dactylopius coccus,* the kermes is *Kermes* spp. (Figure 13).

In Mexico long before the desolation and destruction brought by the Spanish conquest the Aztecs harvested female cochineal insects from Mexico and Guatemala to provide red dye for clothing, decorative hangings as well as for pictograph stories (Figure 14). The Aztec leader, Montezuma, received some of his taxes in the form of cochineal.

The Spanish conquerors expanded the industry and by the early 1800s were exporting hundreds of tons of the scale insects through the port of Veracruz.

The source of food for cochineal is the prickly pear (*Opuntia* spp.). The males are active and fly. Virgin females frequently reproduce without male scales. The female insects bury their long proboscises into the plant tissue, secrete a white woolly covering over their bodies, and lose the use of their legs as these appendages shrink. They spend their lives immobile, reproducing and dying.

The insects are found in the American states along the Mexican border as well as south of the border, and are very abundant in Florida.

Gathering the female scales is a tedious and time-consuming job, and one acre of prickly pear yields around a pound.

Efforts to cultivate the cochineal have not always been successful. Unsuccessful efforts were made in colonial times to establish the cochineal in Georgia and South Carolina. In 1788 the first British colonists going to Australia stopped in Brazil to get the insect and the host plant, to provide a dye source for military uniforms. The insect never became established. The Spanish did succeed in establishing the cochineal industry in the Canary Islands.

KERMES

Well over 3,500 years ago, another scale insect, known to the early Jews as *"tola,"* to the Greeks as *"coccus,"* and today as *Kermes* spp., was used as a red dye source, undoubtedly the principal source of red color referred to in the Bible.

These scale insects are found on an oak of the Near East, in Israel, Lebanon, and neighboring countries, and were harvested by shaking the trees and collecting the insects that fell.

The flourishing dye trade in medieval Holland used kermes, and six-hundred-year-old Flemish tapestries woven with red wool dyed with kermes are still in existence. The insect was successfully cultivated along the borders of the Mediterranean in France and Spain.

LAC

A third source of red came from another scale insect (Figure 15), *Tachardia lacca,* related to the cochineal scale, and called lac. Found in India, Burma, Indochina, and Thailand, the females secrete a sticky substance which fastens them in place on the twigs of certain trees. The twigs are broken off, dried in the sun, and then scraped. In addition to the red dye, shellac is also produced by these scale insects.

15. The lac scale has been used as the source of a dye in India for many centuries and is still of economic value for dye and shellac. The fly has been attracted to a sweet exudate produced by the scale. (*E. S. Ross, California Academy of Sciences, San Francisco, California*)

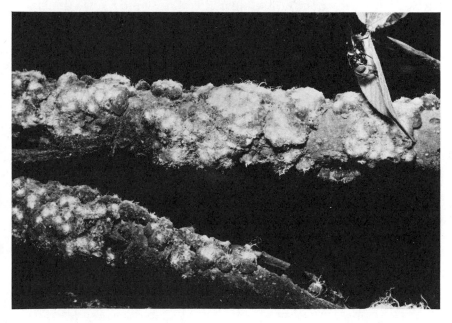

# CHAPTER 2

# Secondary Plant dyes

## ANNATTO

Annatto (*Bixa orellana*), also known among Latin Americans and Puerto Ricans as *achiote,* is a small tree or shrub grown in many parts of the tropical world.

The dark red, spiny fruits split open when ripe, exposing many seeds, each covered with fleshy orange-red pulp, yielding a yellow, orange, or pinkish dye.

The dye is used on cotton, silk, and wool fabrics. It is also used to dye cheese and butter a rich yellow, and in Puerto Rico is used as a saffron replacement for yellow rice, and is fed to chickens to make the yolks darker yellow.

Extraction is by one of two methods (Figure 16). In Mexico the seeds are put in boiling water and left until the coloring matter is extracted. The yield can be increased by forcing the seeds through a screen. Evaporation leaves a thick red paste. Further drying may be needed to aid in preparing the dye for shipping.

In the second method the seeds are mixed with water and allowed to ferment, then macerated, screened, and the water volume reduced by heating. The dyestuff can then be shipped as a paste or block.

Annatto is common in urban grocery stores in the United States in the spice rack area.

It is not soluble in water, but is soluble in the fixed oils and alkaline solutions.

Early users of annatto used warm washing soda as a dip for cotton fabric, followed by a second dip in very dilute sulfuric acid and the dye. The dye was not long-lasting.

16. A West Indian scene in the 1600s showing extraction of annatto dye. The spiny red capsule is on the left, a soaking-fermenting vat is in the center background. The men in the foreground are reducing the pulverized seed coverings to a pulp. The plant is pictured on the right. (*Smithsonian Institution, Division of Textiles, Rita Adrosko*)

### LOGWOOD

Campeachy wood (*Haematoxylon campechianum*), familiarly known as logwood, is a native of Mexico, Central America, and Northern South America, and is still used in Guatemala for a blue color. It lasted in general use in the United States until the 1930s.

The reddish heartwood was chopped, moistened, and allowed to ferment for up to a week. The chips were placed in a cloth bag and put into the dye pot and boiled for a half hour or more, then removed.

A mordant, ferrous sulfate or copperas, was used to give a dark navy blue. Logwood competed with woad and indigo.

### SAFFLOWER

Safflower (*Carthamus tinctorius*), probably a native of Pakistan-Afghanistán, has been used as a dye for five thousand years. Remains of a safflower-dyed mummy cloth have been found in an Egyptian tomb.

It is grown in China, India, Egypt, as well as South America and

Caribbean islands. The seed oil is popular in American grocery stores, particularly for low-cholesterol diets, and is used in India for lamps. The flowers are used to color foods in Spain, the Middle East, South America, and Jamaica.

The flowers yield two colors—red and yellow. The water-soluble nature of the yellow color makes it possible to extract it from the flower heads by crushing them in a sack and washing in a barrel or container of cold water. The remaining red dye could then be removed by dipping into a tank of a weak alkaline solution, such as washing soda.

A major use of the red color was to dye cotton tape used to tie documents—the ill-famed "red tape" beloved by bureaucrats of the world.

## FUSTIC

This yellow, brown, and green dye source, a New World member of the mulberry family (*Chlorophora tinctoria* or *Morus tinctoria*), is usually obtained from trees growing in Mexico, Nicaragua, Jamaica, and Cuba. It is available usually as chips and sometimes as an extract.

The chips were soaked for a few days before using them, to make the dye more available, and were put into a cloth bag during dyeing to protect fabrics from damage.

The dye is color-fast, producing either gold or yellow-tan on wool and a light yellow-tan on cotton. Alum and cream of tartar were used as mordants in the 1800s, but potassium dichromate is preferred now.

## CATECHU, CUTCH

The source of this rich brown dye is a leguminous tree (*Acacia catechu*) native to India and used by East Indians in calico printing.

The dye is obtained from the dark-colored heartwood, cut into chips and boiled to reduce the water volume, and then allowed to evaporate in the sun. It is sold as dark brown chunks.

## SANDERS (*Pterocarpus santalinus*), BARWOOD (*Baphia nitida*), OR CAMWOOD (*Pterocarpus* spp.)

Botanically related, these three red wood dye sources were used interchangeably in the eighteenth and nineteenth centuries, as well as in parts of Asia today.

Sanders is a native of the Philippines, Ceylon, and parts of India; barwood is from Africa.

In India sanders dye is used for facial decorations by women.

The dyes, when imported into the United States in the late 1700s, were considered more suitable for wool than cotton.

## QUERCITRON

The inner bark of black oak (*Quercus velutina*), a native of the Eastern United States, was the source of a yellow dye popularized by an English doctor, Edmund Bancroft, in the 1780s.

The material was used by colonists to dye cotton, wool, and linens, and became an important American export to Europe until the early 1900s.

The inner bark and bark were ground to a fine powder and a mordant of alum and cream of tartar used for a bright yellow dye.

## PERSIAN BERRIES (French berries, yellow berries)

This shrub or tree (*Rhamnus infectorius*) is native to Southern Europe. Related species elsewhere have been used in the same way to produce yellow dye. The wrinkled greenish berries are harvested before they turn red, are dried, and ground to a powder. When used with a tin mordant on wool, vivid oranges and yellows are produced, and on cotton a tan.

## WELD

A small plant, native from Afghanistan and Iran to the Mediterranean basin, weld (*Reseda luteola*) at one time was the principal yellow dye used in England, and has been grown as a crop in Southern Europe. It was apparently used many thousand of years ago in prehistoric times. The dye was extracted in water baths, using the leaves, seeds, and stems. The dye was dilute, and large amounts of the plant were needed.

## SASSAFRAS

The bark and root bark of this aromatic native tree (*Sassafras* spp.) of the Eastern United States was used by settlers to produce rose-tan to rose-brown on wool and shades of gray to dark rose-tan on cotton.

Several mordants, alum, potassium dichromate, and tannin were used. This dye source never gained great popularity.

TURMERIC, CURCUMA

Much used in local diets as a starch source, this Asiatic group of plants (*Curcuma* spp.) with fleshy rhizomes has been used as a source of yellow dye for silk, wool, and cotton. It does not require a mordant, and since it fades easily it has been used mostly in top-dyeing to make greens and browns (Figure 17).

The tubers are used as a spice as well as a highly valued medicinal plant in all parts of Asia. A number of species have been successfully introduced into Latin America with East Indian, Chinese, and Javanese immigrants.

17.   Turmeric, a spice which adds pungency to curry powder, is also used as a dye. (*Ministry of Agriculture, Paramaribo, Surinam, S.A.*)

# CHAPTER 3

# Indian dyes

## Background

The lovely wool weavings of the Navajos, typified in most minds by the Navajo rugs, are a relatively recent art form.

The introduction of sheep by the Spanish about four hundred years ago in New Mexico and Arizona presented a whole new area of creativity to the nomad Navajos.

Among the Western Indians the Pueblo people were noted for their skill in weaving. Using cotton, agave fibers, yucca fibers, and maguey, these agricultural people wove baskets, fabrics for clothes, ropes, footwear, and rugs.

The Navajos adapted Pueblo techniques to the wool of the newly introduced sheep and soon gained recognition as unmatched wool artists. Some old and lovely Navajo rugs contain blue threads, those of army issue overcoats taken from U.S. soldiers in battle.

Navajo women are owners of the sheep flocks and are responsible for designing and weaving. The present flocks still resemble their Spanish ancestors; the sheep are small and sturdy with a low yield of fleece, which is high in hairs quite resistant to dyes. The United States Department of Agriculture has for years worked to improve the quantity as well as the quality of the wool.

## Color Sources

Indian culture is closely tied to the visible world of nature, and the closeness is reflected in the meanings given colors.

red=sun and life                     white=dawn and beginning
yellow, orange=sunset                black=rain, joy

## RED

*Alnus* spp.—alder. Bark used to dye deerskin red-brown.

*Coreopsis cardaminifolia*—coreopsis. Blossoms used for dyeing wool yarn dark red.

*Opuntia* spp.—prickly pear. The fruit is boiled with water, coarse salt, and bark of spruce.

*Rhus* spp.*—sumac. The berries were used for dyeing baskets and for body ornament.

*Rumex hymenosepalus*—canaigre. The large, fleshy tuberous roots are used for a reddish dye as well as for tanning hides.

*Sanguinaria canadensis*—bloodroot. The pounded stems and roots produced a red dye used by Indians as a face paint.

*Iron ores* were used on totem poles and for body painting.

*Animal blood* mixed with animal fat or fish oil was used to color totem poles.

## BLUE

*Delphinium* spp. Petals boiled with rock salt.

*Indigofera leptosepala*—indigo. A native American indigo and urine, after fermenting for two weeks, gave a rich dark blue. The plant is a Western species.

Various berries and fruits.

## BROWNS AND TANS

*Cercocarpus parviflorus*—mountain mahogany. Roots were used to dye baskets, handiwork, and leather.

Bear dung mixed with oils was used on totem poles.

## GREEN

*Chrysothamnus* spp.—rabbit bush. Bark was boiled to produce a green color used in basketry.

Ores of copper mixed with animal fats were a totem pole dye source.

* Sumac, *Rhus* spp., for dyeing should be only those with red-colored clusters of fruits, with flowers appearing after the leaves have expanded. Three very toxic species, poison oak, poison ivy, and poison sumac, have white, tan, or gray clusters of fruits and produce their flowers at the same time as they produce leaves.

## YELLOW AND GOLD

*Chrysothamnus* spp.—rabbit bush. The flowering tops are boiled for about six hours until a decoction of deep yellow color appears. Clay soils rich in alum are heated until pasty and combined with the yellow. The unwashed wool then is immersed in the dye to boil for a half hour.

*Chrysothamnus bigelovii*—rabbit bush. The blossoms are used for dyeing baskets yellow.

*Hydrastis canadensis*—goldenseal. The roots were used as a source of yellow dye.

*Psilostrophe tagetina*—mouse-leaf. Yellow dye from the blossoms is used for painting masks, limbs, and bodies. After the flowers are ground by wives and daughters, the ceremony director combines flower meal with yellow ocher and urine to decorate dancers when assuming the roles of gods visiting in human form.

*Rumex hymenosepalus*—canaigre. Fresh roots are ground and mixed with clay. Cold paste is rubbed by hand into wool yarn. If the wool does not take the color well, a little water is added to the paste and heated. Rich gold color.

*Xanthorhiza* spp.—yellowroot. Roots are used to produce yellow used for baskets and personal adornment.

## PURPLE

Sunflower seed and purple "Indian" corn seed have been used as a dye for baskets and, less frequently, clothing.

*Berberis fremontii*—barberry. Crushed berries are used to color the skin purple.

A number of mordants were used by different tribes as needed. Sumac berries were one, and a mixture of urine and ashes another.

## BLACK

*Castilleja integra*—Indian paintbrush. The bark of the root was used with minerals for coloring buckskin.

*Pinus cembroides*—pinyon pine. Used in combination with bean seeds and sap of poison oak.

*Rhus* spp.—sumac. Leaves and twigs boiled for five to six hours; in another pot pounded yellow ocher is fried until light brown.

Pinyon pine gum, an equal amount, is added to the ocher and stirred to make a paste. It is heated more until it becomes a black powder. The twigs are removed from the other pot and the ocher gum mixed into the water. Wool and leather are died jet black with this compound.

*Charcoal* mixed with animal oils and fats produced black used on totem poles.

# CHAPTER 4

# Methods and Supplies

In dyeing there are four different steps; washing, mordanting, dyeing, and rinsing.

## WASHING

The material is washed before mordanting to remove any dirt or oil that may hinder the dye process. Mix one tablespoon of washing soda with one gallon of warm water (95°) F. and enough detergent or soap to make rich suds. Wash well, and then rinse in one gallon of warm water containing two tablespoons of vinegar. Repeat the rinse, and if the water is not clear, repeat again. Let the material remain in the last rinse until added to the mordant.

## MORDANTING

Many of the natural dyes will fade and "bleed" badly unless the material is first treated with a chemical called a mordant, which helps to fix the color to the fiber. The mordants commonly used with the natural dyes are alum, potassium dichromate, copperas (ferrous sulfate), and tannic acid or some other source of tannin such as oak galls or sumac leaves. Commercial dyers use oils and other substances too difficult for the home dyer to apply.

By using different mordants, a variety of shades and sometimes even different colors may be obtained from one dye. For example, on wool, dahlia flowers used with a chrome mordant give an orange color, and with alum a light yellow. Cochineal mordanted with alum gives red, and with chrome, purple.

Both wool and silk have the property of holding chemicals in their fibers. For example, when wool is boiled in a solution of potassium dichromate, a certain amount of chromium oxide is held in the fibers, and the dyestuff then combines with this mordanted wool to form a permanent color.

Cotton and other vegetable fibers do not absorb the metallic mordants as readily as wool. However they combine well with tannic acid, which is used as a mordant or as an agent for fixing metallic mordants in the fibers.

When mordanting, use only the amount of chemical that the recipe calls for, since too much will damage the material. Simmer only for the proper time, as prolonged cooking may also be damaging.

If the recipe calls for the material to be simmered for longer than thirty minutes, it may be necessary to replace water that evaporates from the pot. Lift the material out on the paddles and add the hot water to the pot. Stir well and return the material to the pot.

In general a mordant is applied before the dye bath.

Remove the material from the mordant bath and squeeze gently. Roll in a towel, and hang up to dry in a dark spot overnight or for several days, as called for. Drying must be complete unless the recipe specifies otherwise. The dry mordanted material is then dampened in warm water before being added to the dye bath.

DYE BATH

Before adding the mordanted material to the dye bath, dampen it in warm water. Then add to the dye bath and simmer for the required time. If any water evaporates, remove the material, add hot water, and return the material to the dye bath.

RINSING

When the material has simmered in the dye bath the specified time, transfer to a rinse of two gallons of water the same temperature as the dye bath. Keep rinsing in successively cooler water until the bath remains clear. Some of the color may wash out in the rinse water, but the color that remains will be fairly fast in the laundry.

NOTES

For all recipes, the amount of material used is one pound. Unless otherwise specified the recipe refers to wool. Do not boil the material, but only simmer. Do not stir in a circle, as this would cause tangling.

The material should be subjected to gradual changes in temperature, as extreme changes cause roughness, harshness, and shrinkage. This is the reason for the first rinse water being the same temperature as the dye bath.

If more than one *mordant* or one *dye bath* is listed under a method, a choice may be made as to which to use. But if more than one method is listed, mordants and dye baths are not interchangeable from one method to another.

If a plant is the source of more than one color, this is listed on the page giving botanical information as "other colors."

When a number of species of the same genera can be used for the same purpose we have listed the plant, for example, as *Quercus* spp., *Betula* spp., and so on. There will be some minor differences in shade from the different species but probably not greater than might be due to using the same species growing in different localities.

Handle all chemicals with care. Alum and sulfuric acid, as well as others, can be poisonous.

## Equipment and Supplies

For home dyeing simple equipment is needed.

Kettles, preferably enamelware. Copper, iron, and tin affect the quality of the colors.

Large pails or tubs if needed, for rinsing the goods.

Gallon and quart measures, cups and spoons.

Cheesecloth or muslin for straining.

Heavy doweling wood or plastic to stir and turn material in the kettles.

A candy thermometer.

Plastic or rubber gloves to protect the hands.

Rubber or plastic apron.

Glass rod.

A clothesline stretched in the shade for drying.

As soft a water as is available.

Battery hydrometer.

Dried plant materials can be bought from supply houses and local drugstores. We have listed a few sources from which materials can be ordered by mail. Chemicals, equipment, and supplies can generally be bought at drugstores and supermarkets.

## Sources of Plant Materials

Bekal Products Company
565 Southwest 22nd Street
Miami, Florida 33135

Capriland Herb Farm
Silver Street
Coventry, Connecticut 16238

Hortica Garden
P. O. Box 308
Placerville, California 95767

Indiana Botanic Gardens
P. O. Box 5
Hammond, Indiana 46325

Nature's Herb Company
381 Ellis Street
San Francisco, California 94102

Local health food stores have
many usable dried roots, barks,
and flowers. Pharmacies can
provide some of the chemicals.

## Plant and Seed Sources

Gardens of the Blue Ridge
Ashford, North Carolina 28603

Lounsberry Gardens
P. O. Box 135
Oakford, Illinois 62673

Harry E. Saier
Dimondale, Michigan 48821

Thompson & Morgan
London Road
Ipswich, 1P2 OBA
England

# CHAPTER 5

# Top-dyeing

Top-dyeing, or dyeing one color over another, is often necessary to obtain a desired color. To the dyer who has a sense of color and color harmony, it offers a fascinating field, but color principles must be followed.

In top-dyeing only good clear colors produce clear colors. If you want a good green, start with a bright, clear yellow, not a muddy yellow or a yellow-tan, and top it with a good blue. Yellows obtained from broomsedge, fustic extract, privet leaves, or goldenrod flowers are satisfactory, but prolonged boiling of any of these is likely to dull the color. Of course, good greens are also obtained by dyeing first with indigo and then top-dyeing with yellow. The combinations possible are almost limitless.

The following chart may be used to gain experience in the basic principles of top-dyeing. Once you have some knowledge of the color principles and techniques involved, you will be able to experiment with different dye combinations for an even greater variety and range of colors.

## TOP-DYEING CHART

| Color Desired | Mordant and First Dye Bath | Second Dye Bath |
|---|---|---|
| black, wool or cotton | indigo method 3 | black walnut (brown) method 2 |
| green, wool | broomsedge (yellow) method 1 mordant 1. Eliminate the afterbath. | indigo method 3 |
| yellow-green, cotton | broomsedge (yellow) method 2. Substitute 1½ tablespoons potassium dichromate for the copper sulphate listed in the afterbath. | indigo method 3 |
| dark green, wool | goldenrod (yellow) mordant 2 | indigo method 3 |
| dark yellow-green, wool | goldenrod (yellow) mordant 1 | indigo method 3 |
| dark yellow-green, wool | hickory (brown) mordant 2 dye bath 1 | indigo method 3 |
| yellow-green, cotton | hickory (brown) mordant 3 dye bath 1 | indigo method 3 |

| | | |
|---|---|---|
| dark yellow-green, wool | chittim bark (brown) mordant for wool, dye bath 2 | indigo method 3 |
| blue-green, cotton | chittim bark (brown) mordant for cotton, dye bath 2 | indigo method 3 |
| red-purple, wool | indigo method 3, no mordant | cochineal (red) method 3 |
| red-orange, wool | broomsedge (yellow) method 1 mordant 1 | madder (red) method 1. Increase the madder to 4 ounces. For a darker color, increase to 1 pound |
| orange, wool | goldenrod mordant 1 | madder (red) method 3. Increase madder to 4 ounces |
| rose-brown, wool | goldenrod mordant 2 | madder (red) method 3 |
| orange, wool | oak (yellow) mordant 2 dye bath 1 | madder (red) method 3 |
| dark coral-pink, wool | oak (yellow) mordant 1 dye bath 2 | madder (red) method 3 |

# CHAPTER 6

# Lichens

The beautiful and sturdy Harris tweeds of Scotland are to this day dyed with lichens, a method used for hundreds of years. The plants are in their own right most fascinating.

Lichens, often thought of as reindeer food, are really two plants living together, each providing some good for the other. Although quite small, each plant consists of a fungus member, lacking chlorophyl, which helps provide moisture, minerals, and protection, and an algae member with pigments required to manufacture organic food.

Lichens are found from the arctic to the tropics, at the seashores on exposed rocks, on mountains with heavy forested slopes, on living as well as dead trees.

The peasants of Sweden, Scotland, Norway, and Ireland use lichens for coloring woolens shades of brown, red, yellow, and purple. They believe that lichens growing on stones give brighter colors than the same lichen growing on trees. August is believed to be the best month for harvesting the plants, as the colors are stronger and clearer at that time.

## BASIC MORDANT

| | |
|---|---|
| Alum | ½ cup |
| Cream of tartar | ¼ cup |
| Water | 2 gallons |

Bring the water to a boil, and add the alum and cream of tartar. Stir well, and add the wet wool. Boil gently for 1 hour. Let the wool cool in the water overnight. The next day hang up to dry.

## Peltigera spp.

The flat and leaflike lichen *Peltigera* spp. is abundant all over the United States and grows on stones and trees. Either yellow-tan or rose-tan may be the final color.

**Yellow-tan**

### DYE BATH

Lichens        1 gallon
Water

Soak the lichens overnight in water to cover. The next day boil for 1 hour and strain. Discard the lichens, and add cold water to the liquid to make 2 gallons. Bring to a boil and add the dampened, mordanted wool. Boil gently for 40 minutes. Rinse and dry.

**Dark rose-tan**

### DYE BATH

*Peltigera* lichens      2 gallons
Water

Dye as directed for yellow-tan. Follow with a bath containing:

Potassium dichromate      1½ teaspoons
Vinegar                   ⅓ cup

Boil gently for 10 minutes. Rinse and dry.

## Usnea florida

This branched, hairlike lichen grows on barks, rarely on rocks, and is broadly distributed over the entire world. On wool it gives a beige color, a yellow-tan, and a dark rose-tan, all with good color fastness.

**Beige**

### DYE BATH

*Usnea* lichens      1 gallon
Water

Soak the lichens overnight in water to cover. The next day boil for 1 hour. Strain and discard the lichens. Add cold water to the liquid to make 2 gallons. Bring to a boil and add the dampened, mordanted wool. Boil gently for 30 minutes. Rinse and dry.

**Yellow-tan**                    MORDANT

> Potassium dichromate      1½ teaspoons
> Water                     2 gallons

Dissolve the potassium dichromate in the water and bring to a boil. Add the wet wool and boil gently for 30 minutes. Hang up to dry.

DYE BATH

> *Usnea* lichens      1 gallon
> Water

Dye as directed for beige.

**Dark rose-tan**              DYE BATH

> *Usnea* lichens      1 gallon
> Water

Dye as directed for beige. Then follow with an afterbath containing:

> Potassium dichromate      1½ teaspoons
> Vinegar                   ⅓ cup
> Water                     2 gallons

Boil gently for 10 minutes. Rinse and dry.

## *Rocella* spp.

This lichen, known as orchil, has been harvested on rocks along the Mediterranean, the Canary Islands, Cape Verde, India, and Ceylon. It has been used for a range of colors from red to blue, and most often for top-dyeing.

This process involved soaking the lichens in fermented urine for a week until a purple color appeared. After 3 or 4 more weeks setting, the unpleasant urine odor had vanished, and the color was a bright crimson. The finished dye was a concentrated paste or block.

The dye was used by mixing with warm water gradually brought to a boil, adding the wool. The dye bath was brought to a simmer, and this was repeated until the desired color was obtained.

## *Cladonia* spp. and *Urcealaria* spp.

This mixture of lichens called cudbear originated in Scotland in the mid 1700s and was much liked in Europe. Available as a powder and made from European lichens, it was exported to the United States but never sold well.

# CHAPTER 7

# Yellow dyes

## ALDER *Alnus* spp.*

**Yellow**

### MORDANT

| | |
|---|---|
| Alum | 1 cup |
| Cream of tartar | ¼ cup |
| Water | 2 gallons |

Dissolve the alum and cream of tartar in the water. Bring to a boil, and add the wet wool. Boil gently for 1 hour. Hang up to dry.

### DYE BATH

| | |
|---|---|
| Alder leaves | 2 gallons |
| Water | |

Chop the leaves, cover with water, and soak for 2 hours. Boil for 1 hour, and strain. Discard the leaves. Add cold water to the liquid to make 2 gallons. Bring to a boil, and add the dampened, mordanted wool. Boil gently for 45 minutes. Rinse and dry.

* See Chapter 13 for botanical information.

## APPLE *Malus* spp.*

**Golden yellow**                MORDANT

| | |
|---|---|
| Alum | 1 cup |
| Cream of tartar | ¼ cup |
| Water | 2 gallons |

Dissolve the alum and cream of tartar in the water. Bring to a boil, and add the wet wool. Boil gently for 30 minutes. Hang up to dry. (2 tablespoons of potassium dichromate can be used instead of the alum and cream of tartar, but boil for 1 hour.)

### DYE BATH

| | |
|---|---|
| Apple bark | 2 quarts |
| Water | |

Chop the bark, cover with water, and soak overnight. The next day boil for 2 hours, and strain. Discard the bark, and add cold water to the liquid to make 2 gallons. Bring to a boil, and add the dampened, mordanted wool. Boil gently for 30 minutes. Rinse and dry.

## ASTER *Aster* spp.

OTHER NAMES: Frost-flower, starwort.

PLANT DESCRIPTION: Leafy-stemmed herbs having lance-shaped leaves with toothed edges. The numerous flowers bear petals of a range of colors, white, blue, red, or purple.

WHERE IT GROWS: It grows in a wide range of conditions in all parts of the United States.

PART USED: Flowers.

* See Chapter 12 for botanical information.

**Green-yellow**

## MORDANT

| | |
|---|---|
| Alum | 1 cup |
| Cream of tartar | ¼ cup |
| Water | 2 gallons |

Dissolve the alum and cream of tartar in the water. Bring to a boil, and add the wet wool. Boil gently for 1 hour. Hang up to dry. (2 tablespoons of potassium dichromate can be substituted for the alum and cream of tartar in the recipe.)

## DYE BATH

| | |
|---|---|
| Aster flowers | 2 gallons |
| Water | |

Chop the flowers, cover with water, and soak overnight. The next day boil for 40 minutes. Strain, and discard the flowers. Add cold water to the liquid to make 2 gallons. Bring to a boil, and add the dampened, mordanted wool. Boil gently for 45 minutes. Rinse and dry.

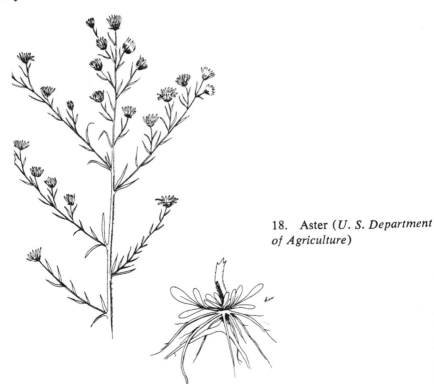

18. Aster (*U. S. Department of Agriculture*)

## BAYBERRY *Myrica cerifera* L.*

**Yellow**                   MORDANT

|            |            |
|------------|------------|
| Alum       | ¾ cup      |
| Cream of tartar | ¼ cup |
| Water      | 2 gallons  |

Dissolve the alum and cream of tartar in the water. Bring to a boil, and add the wet wool. Boil gently for 1 hour. Hang up to dry.

### DYE BATH

|                  |          |
|------------------|----------|
| Bayberry leaves  | 1 gallon |
| Water            |          |

Cover the leaves with water and soak overnight. The next day boil for 1½ hours. Strain, and discard the leaves. Add cold water to the liquid to make 2 gallons. Bring to a boil, and add the dampened, mordanted wool. Boil gently for 45 minutes. Rinse and dry.

## BEDSTRAW *Galium* spp.**

**Yellow-orange**            MORDANT

|            |            |
|------------|------------|
| Alum       | 1 cup      |
| Cream of tartar | ¼ cup |
| Water      | 2 gallons  |

Dissolve the alum and cream of tartar in the water. Bring to a boil, and add the wet wool. Boil gently for 1 hour. Hang up to dry.

### DYE BATH

|                |          |
|----------------|----------|
| Bedstraw roots | 2 quarts |
| Water          |          |

Chop the roots, cover with water, and soak overnight. The next day

* See Chapter 12 for botanical information.
** See Chapter 11 for botanical information.

boil for 1 hour. Strain, and discard the roots. Add cold water to the liquid to make 2 gallons. Bring to a boil and add the dampened, mordanted wool. Boil gently for 30 minutes. Rinse and dry.

## BEETS *Beta vulgaris* L.*

**Yellow**          MORDANT

None required.

### DYE BATH

Beets    1½ quarts
Water

Chop the beets, cover with water, and boil for 2 hours. If canned beets are used, the canned liquid may be added to this water. Strain, and discard the beets. Add cold water to the liquid to make 2 gallons. Bring to a boil, and add the wet, unmordanted wool. Boil gently for 2 hours. Rinse and dry.

## BIRCH *Betula* spp.**

**Pale yellow**          MORDANT

Alum              ¾ cup
Cream of tartar   ¼ cup
Water             2 gallons

Dissolve the alum and cream of tartar in the water, and bring to a boil. Add the wet wool, and boil gently for 45 minutes. Hang up to dry.

### DYE BATH

Birch leaves, dry (any species)    1 gallon
Water

Crush the leaves, cover with water, and soak overnight. The next

* See Chapter 11 for botanical information.
** See Chapter 12 for botanical information.

day boil for 20 minutes. Strain, and discard the leaves. Add cold water to the liquid to make 2 gallons. Bring to a boil and add the dampened, mordanted wool. Boil gently for 30 minutes. Rinse and dry.

## BLACK CHERRY *Prunus serotina* Ehrh.*

**Yellow-orange**                    MORDANT

| | |
|---|---|
| Alum | 1 cup |
| Cream of tartar | ¼ cup |
| Water | 2 gallons |

Dissolve the alum and cream of tartar in the water. Bring to a boil, and add the wet wool. Boil gently for 1½ hours. Hang up to dry.

### DYE BATH

| | |
|---|---|
| Black cherry bark | 2 gallons |
| Water | |

Chop the bark, cover with water, and soak for 6 hours. Boil for 1 hour and strain. Discard the bark, and add cold water to the liquid to make 2 gallons. Bring to a boil and add the dampened, mordanted wool. Boil gently for 45 minutes. Rinse and dry.

## BLOODROOT *Sanguinaria canadensis* L.**

**Yellow-orange**                    MORDANT

| | |
|---|---|
| Alum | 1 cup |
| Cream of tartar | ¼ cup |
| Water | 2 gallons |

Dissolve the alum and cream of tartar in the water. Bring to a boil, and add the wet wool. Boil gently for 30 minutes. Hang up to dry.

* See Chapter 12 for botanical information.
** See Chapter 11 for botanical information.

## DYE BATH

Bloodroot roots      1 quart
Water

Chop the roots, cover with water, and boil for 30 minutes. Strain, and discard the roots. Add cold water to the liquid to make 2 gallons. Bring to a boil, and add the dampened, mordanted wool. Boil gently for 30 minutes. Rinse and dry. (Since this is a toxic plant, we suggest a respirator be used during chopping, and rubber gloves worn.)

## BROOM *Cytisus scoparius* (L.) Link

OTHER NAME:   Scotch broom.

PLANT DESCRIPTION:   A shrub with slender erect branches, growing to 10 feet in height. The leaves are composed of 3 leaflets which are ¼ to ½ inch long, with light hairs. The solitary axillary yellow flowers are ¾ inch long.

19.   Broom (*University of West Virginia. P. D. Strausbaugh, and Earl L. Core.* FLORA OF WEST VIRGINIA. Vols. 1–4. *West Virginia University Bulletin*)

WHERE IT GROWS:   From New England to Alabama, and Georgia, Virginia, West Virginia, Tennessee, and Kentucky. It prefers open, dry areas like meadows, fields, and open glades.

PARTS USED:   Whole plant.

**Medium yellow**         MORDANT

Alum              ¾ cup
Cream of tartar   ¼ cup
Water             2 gallons

Dissolve the alum and cream of tartar in the water. Bring to a boil, and add the wet wool. Boil gently for 1 hour. Hang up to dry.

DYE BATH

Broom plants     2 gallons
Water

Chop the plants, cover with water, and soak for 4 hours. Boil for 40 to 50 minutes. Strain, and discard the plants. Add cold water to the liquid to make 2 gallons. Bring to a boil, and add the dampened, mordanted wool. Boil gently for 1 hour. Rinse and dry.

BROOMSEDGE *Andropogon virginicus* L.

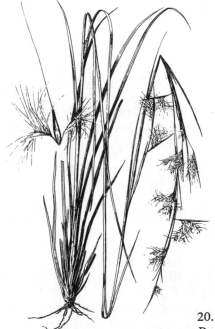

20.  Broomsedge (*U. S. Department of Agriculture*)

OTHER NAMES:   Bluestem, sedge grass, turkey foot.

PLANT DESCRIPTION:   A grass with light green stems later turning brownish yellow, growing 3 to 5 feet in height. Outer blades are 6 to 12 inches long, ¼ inch wide with sharp edges. The flower spikes are covered with hair.

WHERE IT GROWS:   New England, west to Illinois, south to Florida, and Texas. It is a weed of row crops and is found in many different areas.

PARTS USED:   Entire plant.

**Light yellow**

*METHOD 1*

## MORDANT 1

| Alum | 1 cup |
| Water | 2 gallons |

Dissolve the alum in the water and bring to a boil. Add the wet wool and boil gently for 1½ hours. Hang up to dry.

## MORDANT 2

| Muriate of tin | 2 tablespoons |
| Cream of tartar | 2 tablespoons |
| Water | 2 gallons |

Dissolve the muriate of tin and cream of tartar in the water. Bring to a boil, and add the wet wool. Boil gently for 3 hours. Hang up to dry.

## DYE BATH

| Broomsedge plants | 4 gallons |
| Alum | ⅓ cup |
| Water | |

Cover the plants with water, and boil for 20 minutes. Strain, and discard the plants. Add cold water to the liquid to make 2 gallons. Bring to a boil, and add the dampened, mordanted wool. Boil gently for 20 minutes. Transfer to a bath containing the following:

|                        |                |
| ---------------------- | -------------- |
| Potassium dichromate   | 1½ teaspoons   |
| Vinegar                | ⅓ cup          |
| Water, boiling         | 2 gallons      |

Boil gently for 10 minutes. Rinse and dry.

## MORDANT

*METHOD 2*

For wool none required.

|                |                  |
| -------------- | ---------------- |
| (For cotton)   |                  |
| Alum           | 2 cups           |
| Washing soda   | ½ cup            |
| Tannic acid    | 2 tablespoons    |
| Water          |                  |

Dissolve one cup of the alum and ¼ cup of the washing soda in 2 gallons of water. Add the wet cotton, and bring to a boil. Boil gently for 1 hour. Let the cotton remain in the bath overnight.

The next day bring 2 gallons of water to a boil and add the tannic acid. Remove the cotton from the water it has been setting in; squeeze gently and place in the hot bath containing the tannic acid. Boil gently for 1 hour, stirring frequently. Let the cotton remain in the bath overnight.

The next day dissolve the remaining cup of alum and ¼ cup of washing soda in 2 gallons of hot water. Remove the cotton from the water it has been setting in and rinse. Add the cotton to the bath containing the alum and washing soda, and boil gently for 1 hour, stirring occasionally. Let the cotton remain in the bath overnight.

The next day squeeze the cotton out and hang up to dry.

## DYE BATH

|                   |            |
| ----------------- | ---------- |
| Broomsedge plants | 3 gallons  |
| Water             |            |

Cover the plants with water and boil for 1 hour. Strain, and discard the plants. Add cold water to the liquid to make 2 gallons. Bring to a boil, and add the wet, unmordanted wool or the dampened, mordanted cotton. Boil gently for 20 minutes. For wool transfer to a bath containing:

|  |  |
|---|---|
| Copper sulfate | 1½ teaspoons |
| Vinegar | ⅓ cup |
| Water, boiling | 2 gallons |

Boil gently for 10 minutes. Rinse and dry.

## CAMOMILE *Anthemis* spp.*

**Gold**                         MORDANT

|  |  |
|---|---|
| Potassium dichromate | 2 tablespoons |
| Water | 2 gallons |

Dissolve the potassium dichromate in the water, and bring to a boil. Add the wet wool, and boil gently for 1 hour. Hang up to dry.

### DYE BATH

|  |  |
|---|---|
| Camomile flowers | 1¾ gallons (may be fresh or dried) |
| Water |  |

Crush the flowers, cover with water, and boil for 40 minutes. Strain, and discard the flowers. Add cold water to the liquid to make 2 gallons. Bring to a boil, and add the dampened, mordanted wool. Boil gently for 35 minutes.

## CATNIP *Nepeta cataria* L.

OTHER NAMES:    Catmint, catnep, catwort, field balm, nip.

PLANT DESCRIPTION:    A common garden plant with an erect branched hairy stem 2 to 3 feet in height. The heart-shaped, toothed leaves are light green above and hairy below. The white or lilac-colored tubular flowers are only one inch long and grow crowded together at the tips of the stems.

* See Chapter 8 for botanical information.

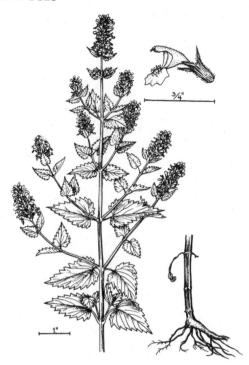

21. Catnip (*U. S. Forest Service*)

WHERE IT GROWS:   It is both a wild plant as well as a garden favorite and is found in Canada and the United States. Catnip is sold by pet shops for the enjoyment of cats. It gained a measure of unusual popularity in California very briefly among some youngsters who thought it might provide "trips" comparable to the deep pleasure it gives cats. For people it didn't work.

PARTS USED:   Whole plant.

**Medium yellow**              MORDANT

| | |
|---|---|
| Alum | 1 cup |
| Cream of tartar | ¼ cup |
| Water | 2 gallons |

Dissolve the alum and cream of tartar in the water. Bring to a boil, and add the wet wool. Boil gently for 1 hour. Let the wool cool in the pot overnight. The next day hang up to dry.

## DYE BATH

Catnip plants     1½ gallons
Water

Chop the plants, cover with water, and boil for 30 minutes. Strain, and discard the plants. Add cold water to the liquid to make 2 gallons. Bring to a boil, and add the dampened, mordanted wool. Boil gently for 45 minutes. Rinse and dry.

## CHITTIM *Rhamnus* spp.*

**Gold**                    MORDANT

*METHOD 1*

Potassium dichromate     2 tablespoons
Water                    2 gallons

Dissolve the potassium dichromate in the water, and bring to a boil. Add the wet wool, and boil gently for 1 hour. Hang up to dry.

## DYE BATH

Chittim berry extract     2 tablespoons
Water                    2 gallons

Dissolve the extract in the water, and bring to a boil. Add the dampened, mordanted wool, and boil gently for 30 minutes. Rinse and dry.

**Yellow**                   MORDANT

*METHOD 2*

Alum                1 cup
Cream of tartar     ¼ cup
Water               2 gallons

Dissolve the alum and cream of tartar in the water. Bring to a boil, and add the wet wool. Boil gently for 30 minutes. Hang up to dry.

* See Chapter 14 for botanical information.

## DYE BATH

Chittim berries, bark, twigs 1 gallon
Water

Chop the plant material, cover with water, and soak overnight. The next day boil for 1 hour. Strain, and discard the plant material. Add cold water to the liquid to make 2 gallons. Bring to a boil, and add the dampened, mordanted wool. Boil gently for 45 minutes. Rinse and dry.

**Yellow chrome compound** MORDANT

None required.

## DYE BATH

(For cotton)
Lead acetate 1¾ cups
Potassium dichromate ¼ cup
Water 4 gallons

Dissolve the lead acetate in 2 gallons of boiling water, and the potassium dichromate in the other 2 gallons of boiling water. Dip the wet cotton first in the lead acetate and then in the potassium dichromate. Repeat 4 times. Hang up to dry.

## CHRYSANTHEMUM *Chrysanthemum* spp.

PLANT DESCRIPTION: An annual or perennial cultivated in flower gardens growing from 1 to 2 feet in height, with flowers that may be pink, red, yellow, white, or purple.

WHERE IT GROWS: Different varieties grow all over the United States.

PART USED: Flowers.

22.  Chrysanthemum
(*U. S. Department
of Agriculture*)

## MORDANT

| | |
|---|---|
| Alum | 1 cup |
| Cream of tartar | ¼ cup |
| Water | 2 gallons |

Dissolve the alum and cream of tartar in the water. Bring to a boil, and add the wet wool. Boil gently for 1½ hours. Hang up to dry.

## DYE BATH

| | |
|---|---|
| Chrysanthemum flowers, yellow | 2 gallons |
| Water | |

Cover the flowers with water and boil for 40 minutes. Strain, and discard the flowers. Add cold water to the liquid to make 2 gallons.

Bring to a boil, and add the dampened, mordanted wool. Boil gently for 30 minutes. Rinse and dry.

## CLEMATIS *Clematis* spp.

OTHER NAMES:   Leather flower, vase-vine.

PLANT DESCRIPTION:   A climbing vine growing to 10 feet in height. The compound leaves are made up of 3 leaflets, 2 to 4 inches long. The solitary flowers grow on a purplish flower stalk.

WHERE IT GROWS:   Pennsylvania, Ohio, Indiana, Illinois, Iowa, Virginia, Georgia, Alabama, Tennessee, Kentucky, and West Virginia. A common garden decorative flower, also found in moist woods.

PARTS USED:   Leaves, branches.

23.   Clematis (*University of West Virginia, from* FLORA OF WEST VIRGINIA)

**Pale yellow**                    MORDANT

| Alum | 1 cup |
| Cream of tartar | ¼ cup |
| Water | 2 gallons |

Dissolve the alum and cream of tartar in the water. Bring to a boil, and add the wet wool. Boil gently for 1 hour. Hang up to dry.

DYE BATH

| Clematis leaves and branches | 2 gallons |
| Water | |

Chop the leaves and branches, cover with water, and soak overnight. The next day boil for 1 hour. Strain, and discard the plants. Add cold water to the liquid to make 2 gallons. Bring to a boil, and add the dampened, mordanted wool. Boil gently for 45 minutes. Rinse and dry.

COCKLEBUR *Xanthium pensylvanicum* Wallr.*

**Lemon yellow**                    MORDANT

| Alum | 1 cup |
| Cream of tartar | ¼ cup |
| Water | 2 gallons |

Dissolve the alum and cream of tartar in the water. Bring to a boil, and add the wet wool. Boil gently for 1 hour. Hang up to dry.

DYE BATH

| Clematis leaves and branches | 2 gallons |
| Water | |

Chop the plants, cover with water, and soak for 2 hours. Boil for 1 hour and strain. Discard the plants, and add cold water to the liquid to make 2 gallons. Bring to a boil, and add the dampened, mordanted wool. Boil gently for 1 hour. Rinse and dry.

* See Chapter 10 for botanical information.

## COMMON MULLEIN *Verbascum thapsus* L.

OTHER NAMES:  Big taper, blanket leaf, candlewick, flannel leaf, ice leaf, Jacob's staff, torches, velvet dock.

PLANT DESCRIPTION:  An extremely woolly plant with a stem 2 to 7 feet in height arising from a rosette of leaves. The small yellow flowers are ⅓ to ⅗ inch across.

24.  Mullein (*U. S. Department of Agriculture*)

WHERE IT GROWS:  It grows in all of the states and large parts of Canada. It is found in dry spots, along railroad embankments, in old fields, meadows, and pastures.

PART USED:  Leaves.

**Green-yellow**   MORDANT

| | |
|---|---|
| Alum | 1 cup |
| Cream of tartar | ¼ cup |
| Water | 2 gallons |

Dissolve the alum and cream of tartar in the water. Bring to a boil, and add the wet wool. Boil gently for 1 hour. Hang up to dry. (2 tablespoons of potassium dichromate can be substituted for the alum and cream of tartar.)

DYE BATH

| | |
|---|---|
| Mullein leaves | 1 gallon |
| Water | |

Chop the leaves, cover with water, and soak overnight. The next day boil for 45 minutes. Strain, and discard the leaves. Add cold water to the liquid to make 2 gallons. Bring to a boil, and add the dampened, mordanted wool. Boil gently for 30 minutes. Rinse and dry.

## CONEFLOWER *Rudbeckia* spp.*

**Light yellow**   MORDANT

| | |
|---|---|
| Alum | 1 cup |
| Cream of tartar | ¼ cup |
| Water | 2 gallons |

Dissolve the alum and cream of tartar in the water. Bring to a boil, and add the wet wool. Boil gently for 1 hour. Hang up to dry. (2 tablespoons of potassium dichromate can be substituted for the alum and cream of tartar.)

DYE BATH

| | |
|---|---|
| Coneflower plants with flowers | 1 gallon |
| Water | |

Chop the plants, cover with water, and boil for 1 hour. Strain, and

* See Chapter 7 for botanical information.

discard the plants. Add cold water to the liquid to make 2 gallons. Bring to a boil, and add the dampened, mordanted wool. Boil gently for 45 minutes. Rinse and dry.

## COREOPSIS *Coreopsis* spp.*

**Orange**                    MORDANT

*METHOD 1*

| Potassium dichromate | 2 tablespoons |
|---|---|
| Water | 2 gallons |

Dissolve the potassium dichromate in the water, and bring to a boil. Add the wet wool, and boil gently for 1 hour. Hang up to dry.

### DYE BATH

| Coreopsis flowers | 1 gallon (or fifteen whole plants) |
|---|---|
| Water | |

Chop the plants or flowers, cover with water, and soak for 1 hour or, if desired, overnight. Boil for 15 minutes, and strain. Discard the plants and flowers, and add cold water to the liquid to make 2 gallons. Bring to a boil, and add the dampened, mordanted wool. Boil gently for 20 minutes. Rinse and dry.

**Yellow**                    MORDANT

*METHOD 2*

| Alum | 1 cup |
|---|---|
| Cream of tartar | ¼ cup |
| Water | 2 gallons |

Dissolve the alum and cream of tartar in the water. Bring to a boil, and add the wet wool. Boil gently for 1 hour. Hang up to dry. (2 tablespoons of muriate of tin can be substituted for the alum. But increase the cream of tartar to ½ cup.)

* See Chapter 11 for botanical information.

## DYE BATH

Coreopsis flowers      2 gallons
Water

Cover the flowers with water, and soak for 3 hours. Then boil for 1 hour and strain. Discard the flowers, and add cold water to the liquid to make 2 gallons. Bring to a boil, and add the dampened, mordanted wool. Boil gently for 30 to 40 minutes. Rinse and dry.

## COTTON *Gossypium* spp.*

**Pale yellow**                MORDANT

(For wool)
Potassium dichromate      2 tablespoons
Water                      2 gallons

Dissolve the potassium dichromate in the water, and bring to a boil. Add the wet wool, and boil gently for 1 hour. Hang up to dry.

(For cotton)
Alum                2 cups
Washing soda        ½ cup
Tannic acid         2 tablespoons
Water

Dissolve 1 cup of the alum and ¼ cup of the washing soda in 2 gallons of water. Add the wet cotton, and bring to a boil. Boil gently for 1 hour. Let the cotton remain in the bath overnight.

The next day bring 2 gallons of water to a boil and add the tannic acid. Remove the cotton from the water that it has been setting in; squeeze gently and add to the hot bath containing the tannic acid. Boil gently for 1 hour, stirring frequently. Let the cotton remain in this overnight.

The next day dissolve the remaining cup of alum and ¼ cup of washing soda in 2 gallons of hot water. Remove the cotton from the pot that it has been setting in and rinse. Add the cotton to the bath containing the alum and washing soda, and boil gently for 1 hour, stirring occasionally. Let the cotton remain in the bath overnight.

The next day squeeze the cotton out and hang up to dry.

* See Chapter 7 for botanical information.

### DYE BATH

|                        |            |
|------------------------|------------|
| Cotton flowers, dry    | ½ gallon   |
| Water                  |            |

Cover the flowers with water, and boil for 25 minutes. Strain, and discard the flowers. Add cold water to the liquid to make 2 gallons. Bring to a boil, and add the dampened, mordanted wool or cotton. Boil gently for 35 minutes. Rinse and dry.

## DAHLIA *Dahlia* spp.*

**Yellow**                   ### MORDANT 1

|                    |            |
|--------------------|------------|
| Alum               | 1 cup      |
| Cream of tartar    | ¼ cup      |
| Water              | 2 gallons  |

Dissolve the alum and cream of tartar in the water. Bring to a boil, and add the wet wool. Boil gently for 1 hour. Let the wool cool in the water, and then hang up to dry.

**Orange**                   ### MORDANT 2

|                        |                |
|------------------------|----------------|
| Potassium dichromate   | 2 tablespoons  |
| Water                  | 2 gallons      |

Dissolve the potassium dichromate in the water, and bring to a boil. Add the wet wool, and boil gently for 1¼ hours. Hang up to dry.

### DYE BATH

|                        |            |
|------------------------|------------|
| Dahlia flowers, fresh  | 2 gallons  |
| Water                  |            |

Cover the flowers with water, and boil for 25 minutes. Strain, and discard the flowers. Add cold water to the liquid to make 2 gallons. Bring to a boil, and add the dampened, mordanted wool. Boil gently for 30 minutes. Rinse and dry.

* See Chapter 12 for botanical information.

## DANDELION *Taraxacum officinale* Weber*

**Light yellow**

None required.

### MORDANT

### DYE BATH

Dandelion roots    1½ gallons
Water

Chop the roots, cover with water, and soak overnight. The next day boil for 1 hour. Strain, and discard the roots. Add cold water to the liquid to make 2 gallons. Bring to a boil, and add the wet wool. Boil gently for 1 hour. Rinse and dry.

## DODDER *Cuscuta* spp.

OTHER NAMES:  Love vine, strangle weed.

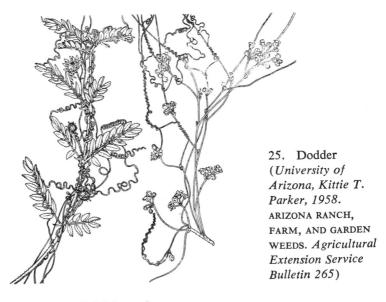

25. Dodder (*University of Arizona, Kittie T. Parker, 1958.* ARIZONA RANCH, FARM, AND GARDEN WEEDS. *Agricultural Extension Service Bulletin 265*)

* See Chapter 10 for botanical information.

PLANT DESCRIPTION: A parasitic, leafless plant with threadlike reddish or yellow stems, with scales rather than leaves. It attaches itself to other plants and twines around them. The small white flowers grow in clusters.

WHERE IT GROWS: Species are found in all parts of Canada and the United States, often as a parasitic weed on grain crops and other plants. It adapts to all kinds of sites.

PARTS USED: Entire plant.

**Yellow**            MORDANT

| | |
|---|---|
| Alum | ¾ cup |
| Cream of tartar | ¼ cup |
| Water | 2 gallons |

Dissolve the alum and cream of tartar in the water. Bring to a boil, and add the wet wool. Boil gently for 45 minutes. Hang up to dry.

### DYE BATH

| | |
|---|---|
| Dodder plants | 3 quarts |
| Water | |

Chop the plants, cover with water, and boil for 45 minutes. Strain, and discard the plants. Add cold water to the liquid to make 2 gallons. Bring to a boil, and add the dampened, mordanted wool. Boil gently for 30 minutes. Rinse and dry.

## ELDERBERRY *Sambucus canadensis* L.*

**Yellow**            MORDANT

| | |
|---|---|
| Potassium dichromate | 2 tablespoons |
| Water | 2 gallons |

Dissolve the potassium dichromate in the water, and bring to a boil. Add the wet wool, and boil gently for 1 hour. Hang up to dry. (¾ cup of alum and ¼ cup of cream of tartar can be substituted for the potassium dichromate.)

* See Chapter 9 for botanical information.

## DYE BATH

Elderberry leaves     2 gallons
Water

Chop the leaves, cover with water, and soak overnight. The next day boil for 1 hour. Strain, and discard the leaves. Add cold water to the liquid to make 2 gallons. Bring to a boil, and add the dampened, mordanted wool. Boil gently for 30 minutes. Rinse and dry.

## EVERLASTING *Gnaphalium* spp.

OTHER NAMES: Balsam pansy, chufeweed, cudweed, fragrant everlasting, many-headed everlasting, old field balsam, sweet white balsam.

PLANT DESCRIPTION: A plant growing from 1 to 3 feet in height with a soft woolly stem, and a basal rosette of leaves, woolly white below and dark green and smooth above. The small flowers grow in the form of heads at the top of the stem.

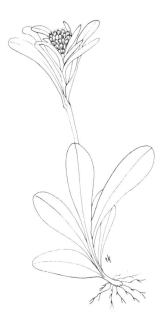

26. Everlasting (*U. S. Department of Agriculture*)

Members are found across Canada and in all parts of the United States, usually in drier spots like clearings, waste places, old fields, and as a garden weed.

PARTS USED: Entire plant.

**Yellow-orange**

### MORDANT

| Alum | ¾ cup |
| Cream of tartar | ¼ cup |
| Water | 2 gallons |

Dissolve the alum and cream of tartar in the water. Bring to a boil, and add the wet wool. Boil gently for 45 minutes. Hang up to dry. (2 tablespoons of potassium dichromate can be substituted for the cream of tartar and alum.)

### DYE BATH

| Everlasting plants, fresh or dried | 3 quarts |
| Water | |

Chop the plants, cover with water, and soak overnight. The next day boil for 1 hour. Strain, and discard the plants. Add cold water to the liquid to make 2 gallons. Bring to a boil, and add the dampened, mordanted wool. Boil gently for 30 minutes. Rinse and dry.

## GOLDENROD *Solidago* spp.

PLANT DESCRIPTION: A coarse plant usually with a single stem, the leaves varying greatly. The yellow flowers are characteristic of most species and grow on flower stalks arising in leaf axils on the upper half of the plant.

WHERE IT GROWS: These plants are found throughout the United States and Canada in a diverse range of habitats.

PARTS USED: Flowers, entire stalk in bloom.

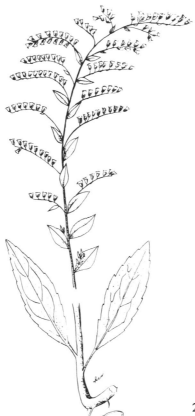

27.  Goldenrod (*U. S.
Department of Agriculture*)

**Light yellow**

## MORDANT 1

| Alum | 1 cup |
| Cream of tartar | ½ cup |
| Water | 2 gallons |

Dissolve the alum and cream of tartar in the water. Bring to a boil, and add the wet wool. Boil gently for 1 hour. Hang up to dry.

**Yellow-orange**

## MORDANT 2

| Potassium dichromate | 2 tablespoons |
| Water | 2 gallons |

Dissolve the potassium dichromate in the water, and bring to a boil. Add the wet wool, and boil gently for 1 hour. Hang up to dry.

## DYE BATH

Goldenrod flowers, stalks with leaves  2½ gallons
Water

Cover the plants with water, and boil for 1 hour. Strain, and discard the plants. Add cold water to the liquid to make 2 gallons. Bring to a boil, and add the dampened, mordanted wool. Boil gently for 45 minutes. Rinse and dry. (The mordant can be eliminated and ¼ cup of alum added to the dye bath just before the dampened wool is added.)

## GOLDTHREAD *Coptis* spp.

OTHER NAME:  Cankerroot.

PLANT DESCRIPTION:  A low-growing plant with shiny 3-lobed evergreen leaves. The small white flowers, ½ inch wide, grow singly on a slender stalk 6 inches high. The roots are yellow.

WHERE IT GROWS:  Eastern Canada to New England, south to North Carolina, Tennessee, and west to Ohio, Indiana, and Iowa. It prefers moist shady spots such as bogs, woods, and swamps.

PARTS USED:  Roots, leaves.

28. Goldthread (*University of West Virginia, from* FLORA OF WEST VIRGINIA)

**Yellow**

## MORDANT

| | |
|---|---|
| Alum | ½ cup |
| Cream of tartar | ¼ cup |
| Water | 2 gallons |

Dissolve the alum and cream of tartar in the water. Bring to a boil, and add the wet wool. Boil gently for 1 hour. Hang up to dry.

## DYE BATH

| | |
|---|---|
| Goldthread roots and leaves | 2 quarts |
| Water | |

Chop the plants, cover with water, and soak overnight. The next day boil for 1 hour. Strain, and discard the plants. Add cold water to the liquid to make 2 gallons. Bring to a boil, and add the dampened, mordanted wool. Boil gently for 30 minutes. Rinse and dry.

## GROUNDSEL *Senecio aureus* L.

OTHER NAMES:   Butterweed, cocashweed, coughweed, false valerian, female regulator, golden groundsel, golden senecio, liferoot, ragwort, squawweed, wild valerian.

PLANT DESCRIPTION:   A plant that grows to 2½ feet in height, is fuzzy when young, but becomes smooth as it matures. The toothed leaves, 1 to 6 inches long, are dark green above and red-purplish below. The yellow-orange flowers, ¼ to 1 inch across, with 8 to 12 petals, usually grow at the top of the stem.

WHERE IT GROWS:   It is found in Eastern Canada south to Alabama, Florida, and Arkansas, and Texas, preferring moist fields and swamps and stream banks.

PARTS USED:   Entire plant.

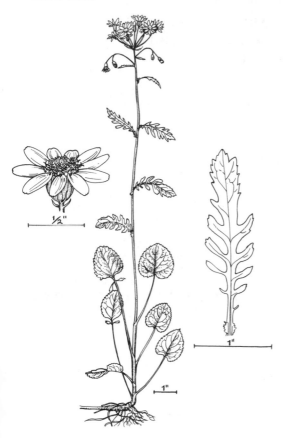

29.  Groundsel (*U. S. Forest Service*)

**Pale yellow**               MORDANT

|                  |            |
| ---------------- | ---------- |
| Alum             | 1 cup      |
| Cream of tartar  | ¼ cup      |
| Water            | 2 gallons  |

Dissolve the alum and cream of tartar in the water, and bring to a boil. Add the wet wool, and boil gently for 1 hour. Hang up to dry. (2 tablespoons of potassium dichromate can be substituted for the alum and cream of tartar.)

DYE BATH

|                    |           |
| ------------------ | --------- |
| Groundsel plants   | 1 gallon  |
| Water              |           |

Chop the plants, cover with water, and soak for 6 hours or overnight. Boil for 30 minutes, and strain. Discard the plants, and add cold water to the liquid to make 2 gallons. Bring to a boil, and add the dampened, mordanted wool. Boil gently for 40 minutes. Rinse and dry.

## HICKORY *Carya* spp.*

**Green-yellow**           MORDANT

(For wool)
Potassium dichromate     2 tablespoons
Water                    2 gallons.

Dissolve the potassium dichromate in the water, and bring to a boil. Add the wet wool, and boil for 1 hour. Hang up to dry.

**Tan-yellow**

(For cotton)
Alum            2 cups
Washing soda    ½ cup
Tannic acid     2 tablespoons
Water

Dissolve 1 cup of the alum and ¼ cup of the washing soda in 2 gallons of water. Add the wet cotton, and bring to a boil. Boil gently for 1 hour. Let the cotton stay in the bath overnight.

The next day bring 2 gallons of water to a boil and add the tannic acid. Remove the cotton from the water that it has been setting in, squeeze gently, and add to the hot bath containing the tannic acid. Boil gently for 1 hour, stirring frequently. Let the cotton remain in this overnight.

The next day dissolve the remaining cup of alum and washing soda in 2 gallons of hot water. Remove the cotton from the pot it has been setting in, and rinse. Add the cotton to the bath containing the alum and washing soda, and boil gently for 1 hour, stirring occasionally. Let the cotton remain in the bath overnight.

The next day squeeze the cotton out and hang up to dry.

* See Chapter 12 for botanical information.

## DYE BATH

Hickory inner bark, fresh (any species)     4 gallons
Water

Chop the bark, cover with water, and soak overnight. The next day boil for 1½ hours. Strain, and discard the bark. Add cold water to the liquid to make 2 gallons. Bring to a boil, and add the dampened, mordanted wool or cotton. Boil gently for 1 hour. Rinse and dry. (For wool the mordant can be eliminated, or, if preferred, the alum and cream of tartar can be added to the dye bath.)

## HORSE CHESTNUT *Aesculus hippocastanum* L.

OTHER NAME:   Common horse chestnut.

PLANT DESCRIPTION:   A large tree growing to 100 feet in height. The compound leaves have 5 to 7 leaflets and are 4 to 8 inches long. The large white flowers are found crowded in clusters on a long flower stalk. The round prickly fruit is about 2 inches across.

WHERE IT GROWS:   Texas east to Georgia and Missouri and north to the higher elevations of Kentucky and North Carolina. It is found as a park and planting specimen as well as wild in wooded areas.

PARTS USED:   Husks, leaves.

**Medium yellow**            MORDANT

Potassium dichromate     2 tablespoons
Water                    2 gallons

Dissolve the potassium dichromate in the water, and bring to a boil. Add the wet wool, and boil gently for 1 hour. Hang up to dry.

## DYE BATH

Horse chestnut husks, leaves     1 gallon
Water

Chop the leaves and husks, cover with water, and soak overnight. The next day boil for 50 minutes. Strain, and discard the plant material. Add cold water to the liquid to make 2 gallons. Bring to a boil, and add the dampened, mordanted wool. Boil gently for 35 minutes. Rinse and dry.

30. Horse Chestnut (*U. S. Forest Service*)

30a. (*Dr. J. Hardin, Department of Botany North Carolina State University, Raleigh*)

# IRONWOOD *Ostrya virginiana* (Miller) K. Koch

OTHER NAMES:    American hop-hornbeam, leverwood.

PLANT DESCRIPTION:    A slender tree growing to 60 feet in height with flaky, furrowed brown bark. The finely toothed leaves are 2 to 5

inches long, oblong to lance-shaped, round at the base, slightly fuzzy.
The flowers are catkins.

WHERE IT GROWS:   It is found from Southeastern Canada as far
south as Virginia, and in high elevations of North Carolina and
Tennessee; it grows in the Western United States to Oklahoma, Iowa,
South Dakota, and Illinois. It likes rich woods and stream banks.

31. Ironwood (*U. S. Forest Service*)

31a. (*U. S. Department of Agriculture*)

PART USED:   Inner bark.

**Orange**                          MORDANT 1

Potassium dichromate     2 tablespoons
Water                    2 gallons

Dissolve the potassium dichromate in the water, and bring to a
boil. Add the wet wool, and boil gently for 45 minutes. Hang up to
dry.

**Yellow**            MORDANT 2

| | |
|---|---|
| Alum | 1 cup |
| Cream of tartar | ¼ cup |
| Water | 2 gallons |

Dissolve the alum and cream of tartar in the water. Bring to a boil, and add the wet wool. Boil gently for 1½ hours. Hang up to dry.

### DYE BATH

| | |
|---|---|
| Ironwood inner bark | 1½ gallons |
| Water | |

Chop the bark, cover with water, and boil for 1½ hours. Strain, and discard the bark. Add cold water to the liquid to make 2 gallons. Bring to a boil, and add the dampened, mordanted wool. Boil gently for 45 minutes. Rinse and dry.

## LILY OF THE VALLEY *Convallaria majalis* L.*

**Green-yellow**            MORDANT 1

| | |
|---|---|
| Potassium dichromate | 2 tablespoons |
| Water | 2 gallons |

Dissolve the potassium dichromate in the water, and bring to a boil. Add the wet wool, and boil gently for 1 hour. Hang up to dry.

### MORDANT 2

| | |
|---|---|
| Alum | ½ cup |
| Cream of tartar | ¼ cup |
| Water | 2 gallons |

Dissolve the alum and cream of tartar in the water, and bring to a boil, and add the wet wool. Boil gently for 30 minutes. Hang up to dry.

* See Chapter 8 for botanical information.

## DYE BATH

| | |
|---|---|
| Lily of the valley leaves, fresh | 3 gallons |
| Ammonia | 1 teaspoon |
| Water | |

Cover the leaves with water, and soak overnight. The next day boil for 1 hour. Strain, and discard the leaves. Add cold water to the liquid to make 2 gallons. Bring to a boil, and add the dampened, mordanted wool. Boil gently for 45 minutes. Rinse and dry.

## MADDER *Rubia tinctorium L.**

**Yellow-orange**          MORDANT

None required.

## DYE BATH

| | |
|---|---|
| Cream of tartar | 2 tablespoons |
| Stannous chloride | ¼ cup |
| Quercitron extract | 2 tablespoons |
| Water | 2 gallons |
| Madder | 1½ ounces |

Dissolve the cream of tartar and ¾ of the stannous chloride in 2 gallons of water. Bring to a boil, and add the wet wool. Boil gently for 50 minutes. Remove the wool, and add the quercitron extract, madder, and the rest of the stannous chloride. Stir well and add the wool again. Boil gently for 40 minutes. Rinse well and dry.

## MARIGOLD *Tagetes* spp.**

**Yellow-orange**          MORDANT

| | |
|---|---|
| Alum | 1 cup |
| Cream of tartar | ½ cup |
| Water | 2 gallons |

Dissolve the alum and cream of tartar in the water. Bring to a boil,

* See Chapter 11 for botanical information.
** See Chapter 12 for botanical information.

and add the wet wool. Boil gently for 2 hours. Hang up to dry. (2 tablespoons of potassium dichromate can be substituted for the alum and cream of tartar, but boil for only 1 hour.)

## DYE BATH

| Marigold flowers, fresh | 2 gallons, or dried | 1 gallon |
|---|---|---|
| Water | (this may include stalks) | |

Cover the plant materials with water, and boil for 1 hour. Strain, and discard the flowers and stalks. Add cold water to the liquid to make 2 gallons. Bring to a boil, and add the dampened, mordanted wool. Boil gently for 30 minutes. Wash in warm soapy water, and then rinse and dry. (If desired the mordant can be eliminated.)

## MOUNTAIN MINT *Pycnanthemum tenuifolium* Schrader*

**Light yellow**

## MORDANT

| Alum | 1 cup |
|---|---|
| Cream of tartar | ¼ cup |
| Water | 2 gallons |

Dissolve the alum and cream of tartar in the water. Bring to a boil, and add the wet wool. Boil gently for 1 hour. Hang up to dry.

## DYE BATH

| Mountain mint plants | 1½ gallons |
|---|---|
| Water | |

Chop the plants, cover with water, and boil for 30 minutes. Strain, and discard the plants. Add cold water to the liquid to make 2 gallons. Bring to a boil and add the dampened, mordanted wool. Boil gently for 30 minutes. Rinse and dry.

* See Chapter 12 for botanical information.

## OAK *Quercus* spp.*

**Yellow**                 MORDANT 1

(For wool)
Alum                        1 cup
Cream of tartar             ½ cup
Water                       2 gallons

Dissolve the alum and cream of tartar in the water. Bring to a boil, and add the wet wool. Boil gently for 2 hours. Hang up to dry. (¼ cup of muriate of tin can be substituted for the alum, but boil only for 1 hour.)

**Yellow**                 MORDANT 2

(For wool)
Potassium dichromate        2 tablespoons
Water                       2 gallons

Dissolve the potassium dichromate in the water, and bring to a boil. Add the wet wool, and boil gently for 1 hour. Hang up to dry.

**Gold**

(For cotton)
Alum                        2 cups
Washing soda                ½ cup
Tannic acid                 2 tablespoons
Water

Dissolve 1 cup of the alum and ¼ cup of the washing soda in 2 gallons of water. Add the cotton, and bring to a boil. Boil gently for 1 hour. Let the cotton stay in the bath overnight.

The next day bring 2 gallons of water to a boil, and add the tannic acid. Remove the cotton from the water that it has been setting in, squeeze gently, and add to the hot bath containing the tannic acid. Boil gently for 1 hour, stirring frequently. Let the cotton remain in the bath overnight.

The next day dissolve the remaining cup of alum and ¼ cup of

* See Chapter 10 for botanical information.

washing soda in 2 gallons of hot water. Remove the cotton from the pot it has been setting in and rinse. Add to the bath containing the alum and washing soda, and boil gently for 1 hour, stirring occasionally. Let the cotton remain in this overnight. The next day squeeze the cotton out and hang up to dry.

## DYE BATH 1

| | |
|---|---|
| Powdered oak bark (any species) | 1 quart |
| Water | |

Soak the bark overnight in 1 gallon of water. The next day boil for 1 hour. Strain, and discard the bark. Add cold water to the liquid to make 2 gallons. Bring to a boil, and add the dampened, mordanted wool or cotton. Boil gently for 30 to 40 minutes. Rinse and dry.

## DYE BATH 2

| | |
|---|---|
| Quercitron extract | 2 tablespoons |
| Water | 2 gallons |

Dissolve the extract in the water, and bring to a boil. Add the dampened, mordanted wool or cotton. Boil gently for 30 minutes. Rinse and dry. For cotton transfer to a bath containing:

| | |
|---|---|
| Potassium dichromate | 1½ teaspoons |
| Vinegar | ⅓ cup |
| Water, boiling | 2 gallons |

Boil gently for 10 minutes. Rinse and dry.

## ONION *Allium cepa* L.*

## MORDANT

| | |
|---|---|
| Alum | ¾ cup |
| Cream of tartar | ¼ cup |
| Water | 2 gallons |

Dissolve the alum and cream of tartar in the water. Bring to a boil, and add the wet wool. Boil gently for 45 minutes. Hang up to dry. (2 tablespoons of potassium dichromate can be substituted for the alum and cream of tartar.)

* See Chapter 8 for botanical information.

**Yellow**

## DYE BATH 1

Onionskins     1 pound
Water

Cover the onionskins with water, and boil for 1½ hours. Strain, and discard the onionskins. Add cold water to the liquid to make 2 gallons. Bring to a boil, and add the dampened, mordanted wool. Boil gently for 1 hour. Rinse and dry. (The mordant can be eliminated and ⅓ cup of alum added to the dye bath just before the wool is added.)

**Orange**

## DYE BATH 2

Red onions     2 quarts
Ammonia      1 tablespoon
Water

Slice the onions, cover with water, and soak overnight. The next day boil for 1 hour. Strain, and discard the onions. Add cold water to the liquid to make 2 gallons. Bring to a boil, and add the ammonia. Stir well, and add the dampened, mordanted wool. Boil gently for 30 minutes. Rinse and dry.

## OSAGE ORANGE *Maclura pomifera* Schneid.

OTHER NAMES:  Bodec, bow-wood osage, hedge, hedge apple, hedge-osage, hedge plant osage, horse apple, mockorange, orange-like maclura.

PLANT DESCRIPTION:  A tree or shrub growing to 30 feet in height with orange wood. The shiny leaves are 2 to 5 inches long, the yellow fleshy fruit 4 to 5 inches around, and hard and dry.

WHERE IT GROWS:  It is found from New England to New York, Ohio, Indiana, Illinois, Iowa, West Virginia, North and South Carolina, to Mississippi, and Georgia. It prefers open sunny areas. It is often grown as a decorative tree.

PART USED:  Extract made from wood.

32. Osage Orange
(*U. S. Forest Service*)

32a. (*U. S. Forest Service*)

**Gold**

## MORDANT 1

| Potassium dichromate | 2 tablespoons |
|---|---|
| Water | 2 gallons |

Dissolve the potassium dichromate in the water and bring to a boil. Add the wet wool and boil gently for 1 hour. Let the wool cool in the pot overnight. The next day hang up to dry.

**Tan-yellow**

## MORDANT 2

| Alum | ¾ cup |
|---|---|
| Cream of tartar | ¼ cup |
| Water | 2 gallons |

Dissolve the alum and cream of tartar in the water. Bring to a boil, and add the wet wool. Boil gently for 45 minutes. Hang up to dry.

## DYE BATH

| | |
|---|---|
| Osage orange extract | 2 tablespoons |
| Water | 2 gallons |

Dissolve the extract in the water, and bring to a boil. Add the dampened, mordanted wool, and boil gently for 30 to 40 minutes. If mordant 2 is used, transfer to a bath containing:

| | |
|---|---|
| Potassium dichromate | 1½ teaspoons |
| Vinegar | ⅓ cup |
| Water, boiling | 2 gallons |

Boil gently for 10 minutes. Rinse and dry.

## PEACH *Prunus persica* (L.) Batsch.

PLANT DESCRIPTION: This familiar farm and orchard plant produces fruit in a wide range of shapes, sizes, and quality. Peach bark is not readily found in lumberyards or organic food stores.

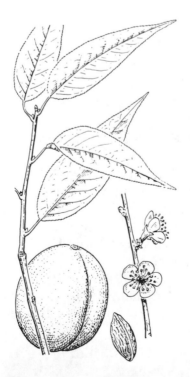

33. Peach
(*University of West Virginia, from* FLORA OF WEST VIRGINIA)

The best place to find some would be on a nearby farm or orchard if you live near a rural area. Sometimes abandoned farms may have old trees. However, be sure that you strip no living tree of its bark without permission of the owner.

WHERE IT GROWS:  It is found all over southern Canadian provinces and all of the United States, including Florida. It is primarily a cultivated tree of farm and garden.

PART USED:  Bark.

**Light yellow**              MORDANT

| Alum | ¼ cup |
| Cream of tartar | 2 tablespoons |
| Water | 2 gallons |

Dissolve the alum and cream of tartar in the water. Bring to a boil, and add the wet wool. Boil gently for 1 hour. Hang up to dry.

DYE BATH

| Peach bark | ½ gallon |
| Water | |

Chop the bark, cover with water, and soak overnight. The next day boil for 1 hour, and strain. Discard the bark and add cold water to the liquid to make 2 gallons. Bring to a boil, and add the dampened, mordanted wool. Boil gently for 30 minutes. Rinse and dry.

## POMEGRANATE *Punica granatum* L.

PLANT DESCRIPTION:  A shrub or small tree growing from 3 to 16 feet in height. The smooth, shiny leaves are 1 to 2 inches long, are oblong to oval. The orange-red flowers are 1 to 1½ inches across. The fruit is brownish yellow to red, and contain a large number of seeds surrounded by a red pulpy juice. The fruits can be stored in the refrigerator for several months.

WHERE IT GROWS:  Originally from the Mediterranean area, it is cultivated in the tropics and subtropics. It is grown in the United

States mostly as an ornamental, but also as a commercial crop in Florida and California.

PART USED:  Fruit.

34. Pomegranate (*U. S. Department of Agriculture*)

## MORDANT

For wool or cotton, none required.

**Yellow-orange**  ## DYE BATH

| | |
|---|---|
| Alum | ¾ cup |
| Cream of tartar | ¼ cup |
| Pomegranates | 3 |
| Water | |

Chop the whole pomegranates or, if desired, mix in a blender with

1 cup of water until well mixed. Add ½ gallon of water, and boil for 20 minutes. Strain, and discard the pulp or fruit. Add cold water to the liquid to make 2 gallons. Bring to a boil and add the alum and cream of tartar. Stir well and add the wet unmordanted wool or cotton. Boil gently for 45 minutes. Rinse and dry.

## PRIVET *Ligustrum vulgare* L.*

**Tan-yellow**            MORDANT

| Alum | ¾ cup |
| Cream of tartar | ¼ cup |
| Water | 2 gallons |

Dissolve the alum and cream of tartar in the water, and bring to a boil. Add the wet wool, and boil gently for 2 hours. Hang up to dry. (2 tablespoons of potassium dichromate can be substituted for the alum and cream of tartar.)

### DYE BATH

| Privet clippings | 2 gallons |
| Water | |

Cover the clippings with water and soak overnight. The next day boil for 1 hour. Strain, and discard the clippings. Add cold water to the liquid to make 2 gallons. Bring to a boil, and add the dampened, mordanted wool. Boil gently for 45 minutes. Rinse and dry.

## ST. JOHN'S WORT *Hypericum* spp.**

**Yellow**            MORDANT

None required.

* See Chapter 12 for botanical information.
** See Chapter 11 for botanical information.

## DYE BATH

| Alum | ½ cup |
| St. John's wort flowers | 3 quarts |
| Water | |

Crush the flowers, cover with water, and soak overnight. The next day boil for 30 minutes. Strain, and discard the flowers. Add cold water to the liquid to make 2 gallons. Bring to a boil, and add the alum. Stir well, and add the wet wool. Boil gently for 45 minutes. Rinse and dry.


## SEDGE GRASS *Carex* spp.

OTHER NAMES:   German sarsaparilla, shear-grass, waldhaar.

PLANT DESCRIPTION:   The numerous members of *Carex* strongly

35.   Sedge Grass (*U. S. Department of Agriculture*)

resemble grasses although not grasses. The flowers are borne on a spike; the leaves are linear.

WHERE IT GROWS: Mostly these 800 plus species prefer moist habitats, but they are found along roadsides, in woods, swamps, meadows, and elsewhere in Canada and the United States.

PARTS USED: Aboveground parts.

**Yellow**

## MORDANT 1

| | |
|---|---|
| Cream of tartar | 2 tablespoons |
| Muriate of tin | 2 tablespoons |
| Water | 2 gallons |

Dissolve the cream of tartar and the muriate of tin in the water. Bring to a boil, and add the wet wool. Boil gently for 2 hours. Hang up to dry. (1 cup of alum can be substituted for the muriate of tin, with a decrease of cream of tartar to 1 tablespoon.)

**Yellow-gold**

## MORDANT 2

| | |
|---|---|
| Potassium dichromate | 2 tablespoons |
| Water | 2 gallons |

Dissolve the potassium dichromate in the water, and bring to a boil. Add the wet wool, and boil gently for 1½ hours. Hang up to dry.

## DYE BATH

| | |
|---|---|
| Sedge grass | 4 gallons |
| Water | |

Chop the sedge grass, cover with water, and boil for 1 hour. Strain, and discard the plants. Add cold water to the liquid to make 2 gallons. Bring to a boil, and add the dampened, mordanted wool. Boil gently for 40 minutes. Rinse and dry.

## SUMAC *Rhus glabra* L., *Rhus copallina* L.*

**Orange**                     MORDANT

|                        |                |
|------------------------|----------------|
| Potassium dichromate   | 2 tablespoons  |
| Water                  | 2 gallons      |

Dissolve the potassium dichromate in the water and bring to a boil. Add the wet wool, and boil gently for 1 hour. Let the wool stay in the water overnight. The next day hang up to dry.

### DYE BATH

|                |           |
|----------------|-----------|
| Sumac berries  | 1 gallon  |
| Water          |           |

Crush the berries, cover with water, and soak for 1 hour. Boil for 45 minutes. Strain, and discard the pulp. Add cold water to the liquid to make 2 gallons. Bring to a boil, and add the dampened, mordanted wool. Boil gently for 30 minutes. Rinse and dry.

## SPRUCE *Picea* spp.

PLANT DESCRIPTION:   An evergreen tree growing from 30 to 200 feet in height, varying from one species to another, with bark ranging from brown to gray to copper. The needles are 4-sided, green to blue-green, packed closely on the branchlets, and ⅓ to ¾ inch long. The cones, which mature in one year, are oblong to cylinder-shaped, usually brown and glossy, and in some varieties can be as long as 5 to 7 inches.

WHERE IT GROWS:   Different species are found in Alaska, Canada, and the United States, as far south as Tennessee and North Carolina. The trees are usually found at higher elevations in open and dry areas.

PART USED:   Cones.

* See Chapter 13 for botanical information.

36.   Spruce (*U. S. Forest Service*)

36a.   (*U. S. Forest Service*)

**Yellow-orange**

## MORDANT

| | |
|---|---|
| Alum | 1 cup |
| Cream of tartar | ¼ cup |
| Water | 2 gallons |

Dissolve the alum and cream of tartar in the water. Bring to a boil, and add the wet wool. Boil gently for 1 hour. Hang up to dry.

## DYE BATH

| | |
|---|---|
| Spruce cones | 1½ gallons |
| Water | |

Break the cones into pieces, cover with water, and soak overnight. The next day boil for 1 hour. Strain, and discard the cones. Add cold water to the liquid to make 2 gallons. Bring to a boil, and add the dampened, mordanted wool. Boil gently for 30 minutes. Rinse and dry.

## SUNFLOWER *Helianthus* spp.*

**Yellow**          MORDANT

| | |
|---|---|
| Alum | ½ cup |
| Cream of tartar | ¼ cup |
| Water | 2 gallons |

Dissolve the alum and cream of tartar in the water. Bring to a boil, and add the wet wool. Boil gently for 30 minutes. Hang up to dry.

### DYE BATH

Sunflowers    1 gallon
Water

Cover the flowers with water, and soak overnight. The next day boil for 1 hour, and strain. Discard the flowers, and add cold water to the liquid to make 2 gallons. Bring to a boil, and add the dampened, mordanted wool. Boil gently for 30 minutes. Rinse and dry.

## SWEET LEAF *Symplocos tinctoria* (L.) L'Her.

OTHER NAMES:   Horse-sugar, yellowwood.

PLANT DESCRIPTION:   A shrub or tree growing to 15 to 18 feet in height. The leaves are toothed, pale green, and fuzzy below. The fragrant yellow flowers appear early in the spring before the sweet-tasting leaves appear.

WHERE IT GROWS:   From Delaware south through Tennessee, Virginia, Florida, Alabama, Mississippi, and Texas. It thrives on damper areas such as swamps and stream banks, but is found in dry thickets as well.

PART USED:   Leaves.

* See Chapter 12 for botanical information.

37.  Sweetleaf
(*U. S. Forest
Service*)

## MORDANT 1

| Cream of tartar | ½ cup |
| Muriate of tin | 2 tablespoons |
| Water | 2 gallons |

Dissolve the cream of tartar and muriate of tin in the water. Bring to a boil, and add the wet wool. Boil gently for 1 hour. Hang up to dry. (1 cup of alum and ¼ cup of cream of tartar can be used instead of the ingredients listed.)

## MORDANT 2

| Potassium dichromate | 2 tablespoons |
| Water | 2 gallons |

Dissolve the potassium dichromate in the water, and bring to a boil. Add the wet wool, and boil gently for 45 minutes. Let the wool cool in the water overnight. The next day hang up to dry.

**Yellow**                    DYE BATH

Sweetleaf leaves, dried or fresh          1 gallon
  (the color is better in the dried)
Water

Crush the leaves, cover with water, and soak overnight. The next day boil for 45 minutes. Strain, and discard the leaves. Add cold water to the liquid to make 2 gallons. Bring to a boil, and add the dampened, mordanted wool. Boil gently for 50 minutes. Rinse and dry.

## THOROUGHWORT *Eupatorium* spp.

OTHER NAMES: Ague weed, common thoroughwort, sweating plant, vegetable agrimony.

PLANT DESCRIPTION: A plant with a hairy stem, growing to 5 feet in height. The paired deep green leaves are 4 to 8 inches long and are

38. Thoroughwort (*U. S. Forest Service*)

up to 1½ inches wide. The tiny white flowers grow in heads containing 10 to 20 flowers.

WHERE IT GROWS:     From Canada, North Dakota, south to Texas, and eastward to New England. It prefers moist, shaded areas.

PART USED:     Flowers.

**Yellow**

## MORDANT

| | |
|---|---|
| Alum | 1 cup |
| Cream of tartar | ¼ cup |
| Water | 2 gallons |

Dissolve the alum and cream of tartar in the water. Bring to a boil, and add the wet wool. Boil gently for 1 hour. Hang up to dry. (2 tablespoons of potassium dichromate can be substituted for the alum and cream of tartar.)

## DYE BATH

| | |
|---|---|
| Thoroughwort flowers | 3 quarts |
| Water | |

Chop the flowers, cover with water, and soak for 1 hour. Boil for 30 minutes, and strain. Discard the flowers, and add cold water to the liquid to make 2 gallons. Bring to a boil, and add the dampened, mordanted wool. Boil gently for 45 minutes. Rinse and dry.

## TICKWEED *Bidens* spp.

OTHER NAMES:     Cuckold, double-tooth, water agrimony.

PLANT DESCRIPTION:     Plants with erect, pale green stems, 2 to 3 feet in height, rough, and hairy. The narrow lance-shaped leaves are toothed. Each flower stalk has one orange flower.

WHERE IT GROWS:     It is found in Southern Canada south to California, Missouri, and the Carolinas, in damp spots such as swamps, and stream banks.

PARTS USED: Entire plant while in flower.

39. Tickweed
(*U. S. Department
of Agriculture*)

**Yellow-gold**                    MORDANT

| | |
|---|---|
| Alum | ¾ cup |
| Cream of tartar | ¼ cup |
| Water | 2 gallons |

Dissolve the alum and cream of tartar in the water. Bring to a boil, and add the wet wool. Boil gently for 1 hour. Hang up to dry. (2 tablespoons of potassium dichromate can be substituted for the cream of tartar and alum.)

## DYE BATH

Tickweed plants      15 to 20 dried or fresh
Water

Chop the plants, cover with water, and soak overnight. The next day boil for 20 minutes. Strain, and discard the plants. Add cold water to the liquid to make 2 gallons. Bring to a boil, and add the dampened, mordanted wool. Boil gently for 30 minutes. Wash in warm soapy water and then rinse and dry.

## TOMATO *Lycopersicon* spp.

PLANT DESCRIPTION:   Although tomatoes are usually a cultivated crop, they have been known to germinate in city streets and sidewalks and vacant city lots. For use in dyeing, it is best to wait until the vines have produced their crop and begin to dry up, which will vary from place to place. In North Carolina ours were still bearing at Thanksgiving.

PART USED:   Vines.

40. Tomato (*U. S. Department of Agriculture*)

**Light yellow**                    MORDANT

| Alum | 1 cup |
| Cream of tartar | ¼ cup |
| Water | 2 gallons |

Dissolve the alum and cream of tartar in the water. Bring to a boil, and add the wet wool. Boil gently for 1 hour. Hang up to dry.

### DYE BATH

| Tomato vines | 1½ gallons |
| Water | |

Chop the vines, cover with water, and boil for 45 minutes. Strain, and discard the vines. Add cold water to the liquid to make 2 gallons. Bring to a boil, and add the dampened, mordanted wool. Boil gently for 30 to 45 minutes. Rinse and dry.

## TULIP TREE *Liriodendron tulipifera* L.

OTHER NAMES:  Basswood, cucumbertree, hickory poplar, poplar, tulip poplar, white wood, yellow poplar.

PLANT DESCRIPTION:  A large tree with unbranched smooth trunk and spreading branches growing to 125 feet in height. The smooth leaves are 3 to 5 inches long and 3 to 5 inches wide, with two lobes at the base and two at the apex. The greenish yellow, bell-shaped flowers have 6 petals with orange markings. The brown, conelike fruit is 3 inches long.

WHERE IT GROWS:  It is found from Southeastern Canada to the Southeastern states, to Florida and Mississippi. It grows in rich soils, near streams, on mountain slopes, thick woods, back yards, and waste areas.

PART USED:  Fresh leaves.

41. Tulip Tree (*U. S. Forest Service*)

**Gold**

## MORDANT

| | |
|---|---|
| Potassium dichromate | 2 tablespoons |
| Water | 2 gallons |

Dissolve the potassium dichromate in the water and bring to a boil. Add the wet wool, and boil gently for 1 hour. Hang up to dry.

## DYE BATH

| | |
|---|---|
| Tulip tree leaves | 2 gallons |
| Water | |

Chop the leaves, cover with water, and soak overnight. The next day boil for 1 hour, and strain. Discard the leaves, and add cold water to the liquid to make 2 gallons. Bring to a boil, and add the dampened, mordanted wool. Boil gently for 30 minutes. Rinse and dry. (The mordant may be eliminated.)

## WHEAT STRAW *Triticum* spp.

PLANT DESCRIPTION: Wheat, one of man's principal food crops, even in ancient times, is grown in many parts of the United States including the West, Midwest, and North Central states, as well as in most regions of Canada. It is a grass family member and is mainly a temperate climate crop.

PART USED: The part used is the straw, which can be gathered or can be bought at farm stores and sometimes nurseries. You may be able to pick up enough around the loading docks of these stores for use in dyeing.

**Light yellow** MORDANT

| | |
|---|---|
| Alum | 1 cup |
| Cream of tartar | ¼ cup |
| Water | 2 gallons |

Dissolve the alum and cream of tartar in the water. Bring to a boil, and add the wet wool. Boil gently for 1 hour. Hang up to dry.

### DYE BATH

| | |
|---|---|
| Wheat straw | 2 gallons |
| Water | |

Cover the straw with water, and boil for 1 hour. Strain, and discard the straw. Add cold water to the liquid to make 2 gallons. Bring to a boil, and add the dampened, mordanted wool. Boil gently for 30 minutes. Rinse and dry.

## WHITE ASH *Fraxinus americana* L.

OTHER NAMES: American ash, American white ash, biltmore ash, biltmore white ash, cane ash, small sod white ash.

PLANT DESCRIPTION: A tall tree growing to 120 feet in height, with toothed leaves 3 to 6 inches long, dark green above, and pale below. The flowers appear before the leaves.

WHERE IT GROWS: It is found from Eastern Canada and New England to Texas, and Florida, often as a park or lawn plant along highways and in moist places.

PART USED: Inner bark.

42. White Ash
(*U. S. Department of Agriculture*)

**Light yellow**

### MORDANT

Alum        ¾ cup
Water      2 gallons

Dissolve the alum in the water, and bring to a boil. Add the wet wool, and boil gently for 1 hour. Hang up to dry.

### DYE BATH

White ash inner bark, fresh      2 gallons
Water

Chop the bark, cover with water, and soak overnight. The next day boil for 1 hour. Strain, and discard the bark. Add cold water to the liquid to make 2 gallons. Bring to a boil and add the dampened, mordanted wool. Boil gently for 40 to 50 minutes. Rinse and dry.

## WILD CARROT *Daucus carota* L.

OTHER NAMES:    Bird's nest weed, devil's plague, lace flower, Queen Anne's lace.

PLANT DESCRIPTION:    A plant with a hairy stem, ranging from 1 to 3 feet in height. The rough, hairy leaves are finely divided, and look feathery or lacelike. The white flowers occur in clusters at the top and are about 4 inches across.

WHERE IT GROWS:    In Canada and in all parts of the United States, it is found in dry sunny spots, like lots, old pastures, and along roadsides.

PARTS USED:    Whole plant.

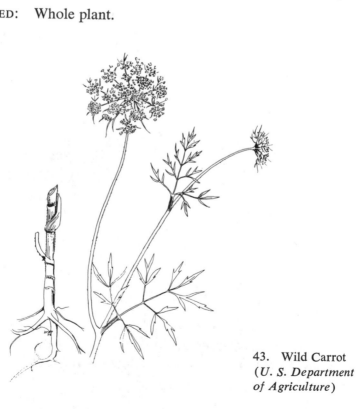

43.   Wild Carrot
(*U. S. Department of Agriculture*)

**Light yellow**                    MORDANT

| | |
|---|---|
| Alum | 1 cup |
| Cream of tartar | ¼ cup |
| Water | 2 gallons |

Dissolve the alum and cream of tartar in the water. Bring to a boil, and add the wet wool. Boil gently for 1 hour. Hang up to dry.

DYE BATH

| | |
|---|---|
| Wild carrot plants | 1½ gallons |
| Water | |

Chop the plants, cover with water, and soak overnight. The next day boil for 40 minutes. Strain, and discard the plants. Add cold water to the liquid to make 2 gallons. Bring to a boil, and add the dampened, mordanted wool. Boil gently for 45 minutes. Rinse and dry.

WILLOW *Salix* spp.*

**Yellow-gold**                    MORDANT

| | |
|---|---|
| Alum | ½ cup |
| Cream of tartar | ¼ cup |
| Water | 2 gallons |

Dissolve the alum and cream of tartar in the water. Bring to a boil, and add the wet wool. Boil gently for 30 minutes. Hang up to dry.

DYE BATH

| | |
|---|---|
| Willow leaves, fresh | 3 quarts |
| Water | |

Crush the leaves, cover with water, and soak overnight. The next day boil for 1 hour. Strain, and discard the leaves. Add cold water to the liquid to make 2 gallons. Bring to a boil, and add the dampened, mordanted wool. Boil gently for 30 minutes. Rinse and dry.

* See Chapter 12 for botanical information.

## ZINNIA *Zinnia* spp.*

**Yellow**

### MORDANT

| | |
|---|---|
| Alum | 1 cup |
| Cream of tartar | 2 tablespoons |
| Water | 2 gallons |

Dissolve the alum and cream of tartar in the water. Bring to a boil, and add the wet wool. Boil gently for 30 minutes. Let the wool cool in the water overnight. The next day hang up to dry.

### DYE BATH

| | |
|---|---|
| Zinnia flowers | 1½ gallons |
| Water | |

Cover the flowers with water, and boil for 45 minutes. Strain, and discard the flowers. Add cold water to the liquid to make 2 gallons. Bring to a boil, and add the dampened, mordanted wool. (The mordant can be eliminated, and ½ cup of alum and 2 tablespoons of cream of tartar added to the dye bath just before the wet wool is added.) Boil gently for 45 minutes. Rinse and dry.

* See Chapter 8 for botanical information.

# Green dyes

## ALDER *Alnus* spp.*

### MORDANT

| | |
|---|---|
| Alum | ½ cup |
| Cream of tartar | ¼ cup |
| Water | 2 gallons |

Dissolve the alum and cream of tartar in the water. Bring to a boil, and add the wet wool. Boil gently for 30 minutes. Hang up to dry.

### DYE BATH

| | |
|---|---|
| Alder leaves | 1¾ gallons |
| Water | |

Chop the leaves, cover with water, and boil for 45 to 60 minutes. Strain, and discard the leaves. Add cold water to the liquid to make 2 gallons. Bring to a boil, and add the dampened, mordanted wool. Boil gently for 35 minutes. Rinse and dry.

* See Chapter 13 for botanical information.

## BLACK WALNUT *Juglans nigra* L.*

### MORDANT

| | |
|---|---|
| Potassium dichromate | 2 tablespoons |
| Water | 2 gallons |

Dissolve the potassium dichromate in the water, and bring to a boil. Add the wet wool, and boil gently for 1 hour. Hang up to dry.

### DYE BATH

| | |
|---|---|
| Black walnut bark | 3 gallons |
| Water | |

Chop the bark, cover with water, and soak overnight. The next day boil for 2 hours, and strain. Discard the bark, and add cold water to the liquid to make 2 gallons. Bring to a boil, and add the dampened, mordanted wool. Boil gently for 30 minutes. Rinse and dry.

## CAMOMILE *Anthemis* spp.

PLANT DESCRIPTION: A branching, perennial herb up to 3 feet in height. The flowers may be white, yellow, or orange, with yellow centers. They grow at the top of the branches and appear solitary or in groups. The leaves are very finely lobed and feathery.

WHERE IT GROWS: Alaska to Newfoundland, Quebec, Minnesota, Michigan, New England, New York, New Jersey, south to Georgia and Florida. In abandoned fields, waste places, barnyards. Widely distributed.

PART USED: Flowers.

OTHER COLORS: Brown, yellow.

* See Chapter 13 for botanical information.

44.   Camomile (*U. S.
Department of Agriculture*)

## MORDANT

| | |
|---|---|
| Alum | 1 cup |
| Cream of tartar | ¼ cup |
| Water | 2 gallons |

Dissolve the alum and cream of tartar in the water. Bring to a boil, and add the wet wool. Boil gently for 1 hour. Hang up to dry.

## DYE BATH

| | |
|---|---|
| Camomile flowers, dried | 1¾ gallons |
| Water | |

Cover the flowers with water, and boil for 45 minutes. Strain, and discard the flowers. Add cold water to the liquid to make 2 gallons. Bring to a boil, and add the dampened, mordanted wool. Boil gently for 45 minutes. Transfer to a bath containing:

| | |
|---|---|
| Potassium dichromate | 1½ teaspoons |
| Vinegar | ⅓ cup |
| Water, boiling | 2 gallons |

Boil gently for 10 minutes. Rinse and dry.

## COPPER

### MORDANT

None required.

### DYE BATH

| | |
|---|---|
| Copperas | 2 tablespoons |
| Copper sulfate | 2 tablespoons |
| Ammonia | ½ cup |
| Water | 2 gallons |

Bring the water to a boil, and add the copperas, copper sulfate, and ammonia. Stir well, and add the wet unmordanted wool. Boil gently for 30 minutes. Remove the pot from the heat, and let the wool cool overnight in the liquid. The next day hang up to dry.

## CHESS WHEAT *Bromus* spp.

OTHER NAMES:   Brome, cheat, chess grass.

PLANT DESCRIPTION:   A grass with upright stems, 2 to 3½ feet in height, downy or hairy with blades 3 to 10 inches long.

WHERE IT GROWS:   It grows in all parts of the United States. It grows in a range of habitats from woods to dry coastal areas.

PART USED:   Flowers.

45.  Chess Wheat
(*U. S. Department of Agriculture*)

## MORDANT

| | |
|---|---|
| Alum | ½ cup |
| Cream of tartar | 2 tablespoons |
| Water | 2 gallons |

Dissolve the alum and cream of tartar in the water, and bring to a boil. Add the wet wool, and boil gently for 50 minutes. Hang up to dry.

## DYE BATH

Chess wheat flowers        3 quarts
Water

Chop the flowers, cover with water, and soak overnight. The next day boil for 30 minutes. Strain, and discard the flowers. Add cold water to the liquid to make 2 gallons. Bring to a boil, and add the dampened, mordanted wool. Boil gently for 30 minutes. Rinse and dry.

## CONEFLOWER *Rudbeckia triloba* L.

OTHER NAMES:   Brown-eyed susan, eye daisy, darkey head, yellow daisy.

PLANT DESCRIPTION:   A bright green, smooth, plant growing to 5 feet in height. The leaves are ovate to lance-shaped with 3 or more lobes coarsely toothed. The flower is made up of yellow rays with a dark brown base and a purple center. Close relatives resemble this one greatly.

46.  Coneflower (*U. S. Department of Agriculture*)

WHERE IT GROWS:    They are concentrated east of the Mississippi and are found in New York, New Jersey, west to Minnesota and Oklahoma, south to Tennessee, Georgia, Louisiana, Arkansas, Texas. Some prefer woods and stream banks, others dry woods, fields, and waste areas.

PART USED:    Flowers.

OTHER COLOR:    Yellow.

## MORDANT

| Alum | 1 cup |
| Cream of tartar | ¼ cup |
| Water | 2 gallons |

Dissolve the alum and cream of tartar in the water. Bring to a boil, and add the wet wool. Boil gently for 1 hour. Hang up to dry.

## DYE BATH

| Coneflowers (fresh or dried) | 3 quarts |
| Water | |
| Copperas | 2 teaspoons |

Cover the flowers with water, and boil for 35 minutes. Strain, and discard the flowers. Add cold water to the liquid to make 2 gallons. Bring to a boil, and add the copperas. Stir well, and add the dampened, mordanted wool. Boil gently for 1 hour. Rinse and dry.

## GIANT CANE *Arundinaria gigantea* (Walt.) Muhl.

OTHER NAME:    Large cane.

PLANT DESCRIPTION:    A coarse perennial with bamboolike stems, growing to 6½ feet in height. The leaves are lance-shaped, ⅓ to 1½ inches long. The sheaths are hairy.

WHERE IT GROWS:    Eastern United States south to Florida and west to Texas and Missouri, usually in moist areas like stream banks and swamps.

PARTS USED:  Leaves.

47.  Giant Cane (*U. S. Department of Agriculture*)

## MORDANT

| Alum | ¾ cup |
|---|---|
| Cream of tartar | ¼ cup |
| Water | 2 gallons |

Dissolve the alum and cream of tartar in the water, and bring to a boil. Add the wet wool, and boil gently for 50 minutes. Hang up to dry.

## DYE BATH

| Giant cane leaves | 2 gallons |
|---|---|
| Water | |

Chop the leaves, cover with water, and soak overnight. The next day boil for 40 minutes. Strain, and discard the leaves. Add cold water to the liquid to make 2 gallons. Bring to a boil, and add the dampened, mordanted wool. Boil gently for 45 minutes. Rinse and dry.

## HOLLYHOCK *Althaea rosea* Cav.*

### MORDANT

| | |
|---|---|
| Alum | ½ cup |
| Cream of tartar | ¼ cup |
| Water | 2 gallons |

Dissolve the alum and cream of tartar in the water. Bring to a boil, and add the wet wool. Boil gently for 30 minutes. Hang up to dry.

### DYE BATH

| | |
|---|---|
| Hollyhock leaves | 2 gallons |
| Ammonia | 1 teaspoon |
| Water | |

Chop the leaves, cover with water, and soak overnight. The next day boil for 1 hour, and strain. Discard the leaves, and add cold water to the liquid to make 2 gallons. Bring to a boil, and add the ammonia. Stir well and add the dampened, mordanted wool. Boil gently for 30 minutes. Rinse and dry.

## IRIS *Iris* spp.

PLANT DESCRIPTION:   A perennial with a bulb, or rhizome, and an erect stem which may be simple or branched. The leaves are blade-like. The single large flowers which appear at the top of the plant are of many colors.

WHERE IT GROWS:   In all parts of Canada and the United States, where it is frequently in cultivated flower gardens. It is found wild in wet places as well as in dry woods.

PART USED:   Fresh purple flowers.

* See Chapter 11 for botanical information.

48. Iris (*U. S. Department of Agriculture*)

## MORDANT

| | |
|---|---|
| Nickel sulfate | ¼ cup |
| Potassium dichromate | ¼ cup |
| Water | 2 gallons |

Dissolve the nickel sulfate and potassium dichromate in the water. Bring to a boil, and add the wet wool. Boil gently for 1 hour. Hang up to dry.

## DYE BATH

| | |
|---|---|
| Purple iris flowers, fresh | 3 quarts |
| Water | |

Chop the irises, cover with water, and boil for 30 minutes. Strain, and discard the flowers. Add cold water to the liquid to make 2 gallons. Bring to a boil, and add the dampened, mordanted wool. Boil gently for 30 minutes. Rinse and dry.

## LILY OF THE VALLEY *Convallaria majalis* L.

PLANT DESCRIPTION:    A small plant with oblong to oval leaves 4 to 8 inches long. The white, highly fragrant flowers are ⅜ inch across, in clusters.

WHERE IT GROWS:    Usually grown in gardens all over the United States, and found wild in a range of sites.

PART USED:    Fresh leaves.

OTHER COLOR:    Yellow.

49. Lily of the Valley (*U. S. Department of Agriculture*)

## MORDANT

| | |
|---|---|
| Alum | 1 cup |
| Cream of tartar | ¼ cup |
| Water | 2 gallons |

Dissolve the alum and cream of tartar in the water. Bring to a boil and add the wet wool. Boil gently for 30 minutes. Hang up to dry. (The cream of tartar can be eliminated and the wool boiled for 1 hour.)

## DYE BATH

Lily of the valley leaves      2 gallons
Water

Crush the leaves, cover with water, and soak overnight. The next day boil for 1 hour. Strain, and discard the leaves. Add cold water to the liquid to make 2 gallons. Bring to a boil, and add the dampened, mordanted wool. Boil gently for 30 minutes. Rinse and dry.

## MISTLETOE *Phoradeondron serotinum* (Ref.) M. C. Johnston

OTHER NAMES:    American mistletoe, Christmas mistletoe.

PLANT DESCRIPTION:    A very familiar small, clumplike parasitic plant growing on flowering trees. The small, roundish light green leaves are heavy and thick. Everyone is familiar with the white berries growing in clusters.

50. Mistletoe (*University of West Virginia, from* FLORA OF WEST VIRGINIA)

WHERE IT GROWS:    This species is found from Texas and Florida north to Minnesota, Wisconsin, and Michigan and east to Pennsylvania, New Jersey, and New England. It prefers lower elevations.

PARTS USED:    Whole plant minus berries.

## MORDANT

| | |
|---|---|
| Alum | 1 cup |
| Cream of tartar | 2 tablespoons |
| Water | 2 gallons |

Dissolve the alum and cream of tartar in the water. Bring to a boil, and add the wet wool. Boil gently for 1 hour. Hang up to dry. If desired, 2 tablespoons of potassium dichromate may be used instead of the alum and cream of tartar in the above recipe.

## DYE BATH

| | |
|---|---|
| Mistletoe | 1½ gallons |
| Water | |

Chop the mistletoe, cover with water, and boil for 30 minutes. Strain, and discard the mistletoe. Add cold water to the liquid to make 2 gallons. Bring to a boil, and add the dampened, mordanted wool. Boil gently for 45 minutes. Rinse and dry.

## MORNING GLORY *Ipomoea* spp.

OTHER NAMES:    Blue dawn flower, wild sweet potato.

PLANT DESCRIPTION:    Most familiar is the morning glory, a climbing twiner with alternate leaves and large purple flowers. There are domesticated varieties with double flowers and flowers of many colors. The sweet potato is a close relative. The wild sweet potato has edible roots.

WHERE IT GROWS:    Relatives are found in all parts of Canada and the United States, often as weeds in vegetable gardens, along fence rows, in row crops, and orchards.

PART USED:    Fresh flowers.

51. Morning Glory
(*University of West Virginia,
from* FLORA OF WEST
VIRGINIA)

## MORDANT

None required.

## DYE BATH

| | |
|---|---|
| Morning glory blossoms, fresh | 2 gallons |
| Alum | ½ cup |
| Cream of tartar | ¼ cup |
| Water | 2 gallons |

Cover the flowers with water, and boil for 45 minutes. Strain and discard the flowers. Add cold water to the liquid to make 2 gallons. Bring to a boil, and add the alum and cream of tartar. Stir well, and add the wet wool. Boil gently for 30 minutes. Rinse and dry.

## NETTLE *Urtica dioica* L.

OTHER NAMES:    Great nettle, singing nettle, slender nettle, tall nettle.

PLANT DESCRIPTION:    A rather rough plant with a stem covered with unpleasant irritating hairs, growing from 2 to 4 feet in height. The long oval leaves, 2 to 3 inches wide and 3 to 6 inches long, come to a point and are toothed. The lower leaves are heart-shaped. The small green flowers grow in clusters toward the top of the plant. Other, closely related species are fairly common.

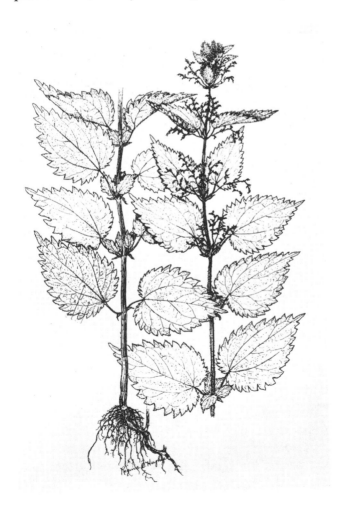

52. Nettle (*U. S. Department of Agriculture*)

WHERE IT GROWS: It occurs from Southern Canada to New England, west to Illinois, Minnesota, south to Missouri, and Virginia, North and South Carolina, and West Virginia, in dry places, roadsides, and old fields.

PARTS USED: Roots, stalks, leaves.

## MORDANT

| | |
|---|---|
| Alum | 1 cup |
| Cream of tartar | ¼ cup |
| Water | 2 gallons |

Dissolve the alum and cream of tartar in the water. Bring to a boil, and add the wet wool. Boil gently for 30 minutes. Hang up to dry.

## DYE BATH

| | |
|---|---|
| Nettle roots, stalks, leaves | 1½ gallons |
| Water | |

Crush the plant materials, cover with water, and soak overnight. The next day boil for 1 hour. Strain and discard the plant materials. Add cold water to the liquid to make 2 gallons. Bring to a boil, and add the dampened, mordanted wool. Boil gently for 30 minutes. Rinse and dry.

## OAK *Quercus* spp.*

## MORDANT

| | |
|---|---|
| Potassium dichromate | 2 tablespoons |
| Water | 2 gallons |

Dissolve the potassium dichromate in the water, and bring to a boil. Add the wet wool, and boil gently for 1 hour. Hang up to dry.

## DYE BATH

| | |
|---|---|
| Oak bark (any species) | 3 gallons |
| Water | |

Chop the bark, cover with water, and soak overnight. The next

* See Chapter 10 for botanical information.

day boil for 2 hours and strain. Discard the bark, and add cold water to the liquid to make 2 gallons. Bring to a boil, and add the dampened, mordanted wool. Boil gently for 30 minutes. Rinse and dry.

## ONION *Allium cepa* L.

PLANT DESCRIPTION:   A common garden plant, annual or biennial, with large bulbs. The leaves are hollow, sea green, and tapering. The flower stalk is 2 to 4 feet tall, much taller than the leaves; the white or lilac flowers occur in large numbers.

WHERE IT GROWS:   Wherever man is found, except in the arctic, onions and their relatives are grown.

PARTS USED:   Outer skins, whole dried onions.

OTHER COLOR:   Yellow.

### MORDANT

| | |
|---|---|
| Alum | ½ cup |
| Cream of tartar | ¼ cup |
| Water | 2 gallons |

Dissolve the alum and cream of tartar in the water, and bring to a boil. Add the wet wool, and boil gently for 30 minutes. Hang up to dry.

### DYE BATH

| | |
|---|---|
| Onions, whole | 5 large |
| Water | |

Slice the onions without peeling, cover with water, and soak overnight. The next day boil for 1 hour. Strain, and discard the onion. Add cold water to the liquid to make 2 gallons, and bring to a boil. Add the dampened, mordanted wool, and boil gently for 1 hour. Rinse and dry.

1. Indigo was much used in colonial times for clothes, curtains, and bedding. This light blue overshot coverlet is made of two shades of blue wool and natural linen. It was made in Stonington, Connecticut, probably in the late 1700's. (*Smithsonian Institution, Division of Textiles, Rita Adrosko*)

2. and 3.   These are two lovely examples of Hopi Indian basket weaving. The upper is a basket by Stella Preston. The purple color is a dye made from Indian corn, and the yellow color comes from the flowers of rabbit bush. The lower is a wall plaque, the work of Dora Tawahongva. *(Exxon, U.S.A., and Don Dedera, Del Mar, California)*

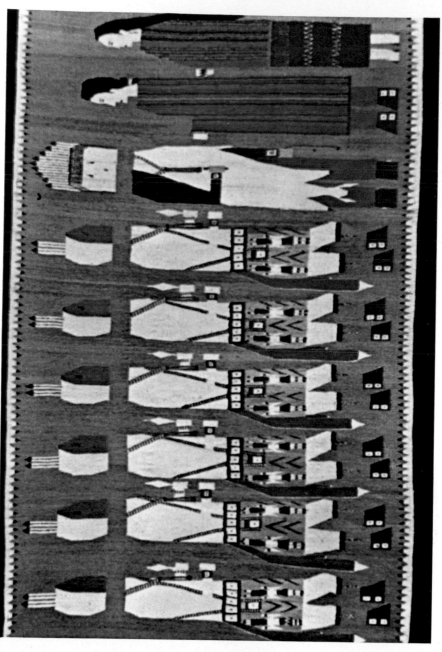

4. Beginning about 1700 the Navajo people learned the art of weaving from the Pueblos. In the Pueblo world the men have been the weavers, but among the Navajo, women took up the task. This wall hanging by Della Woody is of the *yei-bei-chai* ceremony, a tradition of great age in which dancers impersonate visiting yei deities who free the home from sickness. *(Photo Bureau of Indian Affairs)*

5. This weaving, a rug done in the "Chief's blanket" design, is a contemporary version of a classic pattern combining striped and stepped motifs. *(Photo Bureau of Indian Affairs)*

## PARSLEY *Petroselinum crispum* Nym.

PLANT DESCRIPTION: This rather short, branching, curly-leaved herb, used mostly for garnishing and flavoring, is available year round fresh. A cultivated crop, most of it is grown in the South, where it can be grown as a winter crop, and in the West.

PART USED: Fresh leaves.

53. Parsley
(Curled and Plain)
(*U. S. Department of Agriculture*)

### MORDANT

| | |
|---|---|
| Alum | ½ cup |
| Cream of tartar | ¼ cup |
| Water | 2 gallons |

Dissolve the alum and cream of tartar in the water. Bring to a boil, and add the wet wool. Boil gently for 30 minutes. Hang up to dry.

## DYE BATH

Parsley     2 quarts
Water

Chop the parsley, cover with water, and boil for 1 hour. Strain, and discard the parsley. Add cold water to the liquid to make 2 gallons. Bring to a boil, and add the dampened, mordanted wool. Boil gently for 1 hour. Rinse and dry.

## PLANTAIN *Plantago* spp.

OTHER NAMES:  Buckhorn, fleaseed, psyllium, ribgrass, ribwort, ripplegrass, whitemans foot.

54.  Plantain (*U. S. Department of Agriculture*)

PLANT DESCRIPTION: A low-growing plant with leaves ranging from narrow and grasslike to broadly elliptical, with conspicuous ribs. Flowers in tall species sometimes grow on stalks 3 feet in height.

WHERE IT GROWS: Many plantains are found in Canada and the United States, mostly in fields, lawns, roadsides, and at the edges of woods. Some are found in swamps and in lakes and ponds.

PARTS USED: Leaves, roots.

## MORDANT

| | |
|---|---|
| Alum | 1 cup |
| Cream of tartar | ¼ cup |
| Water | 2 gallons |

Dissolve the alum and cream of tartar in the water. Bring to a boil, and add the wool. Boil gently for 1 hour. Hang up to dry.

## DYE BATH

| | |
|---|---|
| Plantain leaves, roots | 1½ gallons |
| Water | |

Chop the plant material, cover with water, and soak overnight. The next day boil for 1 hour. Strain, and discard the plant material. Add cold water to the liquid to make 2 gallons. Bring to a boil, and add the dampened, mordanted wool. Boil gently for 30 minutes. Rinse and dry.

# RAGWEED *Ambrosia* spp.

OTHER NAMES: Crownweed, hog-weed, horseweed, mayweed.

PLANT DESCRIPTION: An annual herb, with some species growing to 10 feet in height while others grow to only 3 feet. The lobed leaves have finely toothed edges and resemble carrot or fennel. The tiny flowers are borne on spikes up to 6 inches long toward the top of the plant.

WHERE IT GROWS: Across Southern Canada, and in almost every state of the U.S. In fields, pastures, glades, waste areas, low ground.

PARTS USED: Whole plant.

55. Ragweed (*U. S. Department of Agriculture*)

## MORDANT

| | |
|---|---|
| Alum | 1 cup |
| Cream of tartar | ¼ cup |
| Water | 2 gallons |

Dissolve the alum and cream of tartar in the water. Bring to a boil, and add the wet wool. Boil gently for 1 hour. Hang up to dry.

## DYE BATH

Ragweed, whole plant     2 gallons
Water

Chop the plants, cover with water, and soak overnight. The next day boil for 40 minutes. Strain, and discard the plants. Add cold water to the liquid to make 2 gallons. Bring to a boil, and add the dampened, mordanted wool. Boil gently for 35 minutes. Rinse and dry.

## RED CEDAR *Juniperus virginiana* L.*

## MORDANT

Ammonium chloride     3 tablespoons
Alum                  ½ cup
Cream of tartar       ¼ cup
Copper sulfate        ¼ cup
Water                 2 gallons

Dissolve the ammonium chloride, alum, cream of tartar, and copper sulfate in the water. Bring to a boil, and add the wet wool. Boil gently for 1½ hours. Hang up to dry.

## DYE BATH

Red cedar berries, ripe     2 quarts
Copper acetate              ¼ cup
Water

Crush the cedar berries, cover with water, and soak overnight. The next day boil for 45 minutes. Strain, and discard the pulp. Add cold water to the liquid to make 2 gallons. Bring to a boil, and add the copper acetate. Stir well, and add the dampened, mordanted wool. Boil gently for 25 minutes. Rinse and dry.

* See Chapter 10 for botanical information.

## SMARTWEED *Polygonum hydropiper* L.

OTHER NAMES: Bite-tongue, biting knotweed, common smartweed, red knees, red-shanks, shakeweed, sickle weed, water pepper.

PLANT DESCRIPTION: The plant has a smooth, erect, slender stem, light green to reddish, growing to 2 feet in height. The smooth, narrow, lance-shaped leaves range from 1 to 4 inches long with wavy edges. The greenish tiny flowers grow on flower stalks which grow from the leaf stems.

WHERE IT GROWS: It grows throughout North America in a great variety of habitats including wet areas, gardens, roadsides, lawns, gardens, and old fields.

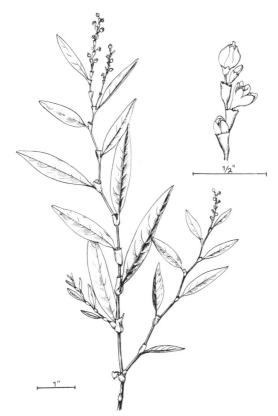

½"

1"

56. Smartweed (*U. S. Forest Service*)

## MORDANT

None required.

## DYE BATH

| | |
|---|---|
| Smartweed, entire plant | 3 gallons |
| Alum | ½ cup |
| Water | |

Chop the smartweed, cover with water, and boil for 2 hours. Strain, and discard the smartweed. Add cold water to the liquid to make 2 gallons, and add the alum. Bring to a boil, and add the wet, unmordanted wool. Boil gently for 30 minutes. Rinse and dry.

## SOURWOOD *Nyssa sylvatica* Marsh.*

## MORDANT

| | |
|---|---|
| Alum | 1 cup |
| Cream of tartar | ¼ cup |
| Water | 2 gallons |

Dissolve the alum and cream of tartar in the water. Bring to a boil, and add the wet wool. Boil gently for 1 hour. Hang up to dry.

## DYE BATH

| | |
|---|---|
| Sourwood bark | 2½ gallons |
| Water | |

Chop the bark, cover with water, and soak overnight. The next day boil for 2 hours and strain. Discard the bark, and add cold water to the liquid to make 2 gallons. Bring to a boil, and add the dampened, mordanted wool. Boil gently for 30 minutes. Transfer to a bath containing:

| | |
|---|---|
| Potassium dichromate | 1½ teaspoons |
| Vinegar | ⅓ cup |
| Water | 2 gallons |

Boil gently for 10 minutes. Rinse and dry.

* See Chapter 13 for botanical information.

## SPINACH *Spinacia* spp.

PLANT DESCRIPTION:    Native of China, this familiar green can be bought fresh, canned, or frozen. If the canned is used, the liquid from the can many be added to the dye bath.

### MORDANT

| | |
|---|---|
| Alum | ½ cup |
| Cream of tartar | ¼ cup |
| Water | 2 gallons |

Dissolve the alum and cream of tartar, and bring to a boil. Add the wet wool, and boil gently for 30 minutes. Hang up to dry.

### DYE BATH

| | |
|---|---|
| Spinach | 1 gallon |
| Water | |

Chop the spinach, cover with water and boil for 30 minutes. Strain, and discard the spinach. Add cold water to the liquid to make 2 gallons. Bring to a boil, and add the dampened, mordanted wool. Boil gently for 1 hour. Rinse and dry.

## YARROW *Achillea millefolium* L.*

### MORDANT

None required.

### DYE BATH

| | |
|---|---|
| Yarrow leaves | 1½ gallons |
| Copperas | 1 teaspoon |
| Water | |

Chop the yarrow leaves, cover with water, and boil for 45 minutes. Strain, and discard the leaves. Add cold water to the liquid to make

* See Chapter 14 for botanical information,

2 gallons, and bring to a boil. Add the copperas and stir well. Add the wet unmordanted wool, and boil gently for 45 minutes. Rinse and dry.

## ZINNIA *Zinnia* spp.

PLANT DESCRIPTION: A popular annual grown in flower gardens all over the United States, growing to 1 foot in height with long-lasting bright yellow or orange flowers.

PART USED: Flowers.

57. Zinnia (*U. S. Department of Agriculture*)

## MORDANT

Potassium dichromate     2 tablespoons
Water                    2 gallons

Dissolve the potassium dichromate in the water, and bring to a boil. Add the wet wool, and boil gently for 1 hour. Let the wool cool in the water, and then hang up to dry.

## DYE BATH

Zinnia flowers, fresh     1½ gallons
Water

Cover the flowers with water, and boil for 20 minutes. Strain, and discard the flowers. Add cold water to the liquid to make 2 gallons. Bring to a boil, and add the dampened, mordanted wool. Boil gently for 30 minutes. Rinse and dry.

# CHAPTER 9

# Blue dyes

## BLUEBERRY *Vaccinium* spp.

OTHER NAMES: Bilberry, cranberry, deerberry, huckleberry, spar-kleberry, whortleberry.

PLANT DESCRIPTION: An erect or creeping shrub growing from 1 to 12 feet in height. The leaves are oval to oblong, and pointed. The clusters of small flowers are white or greenish to pink. The small round berry is reddish brown to a dark blue or black.

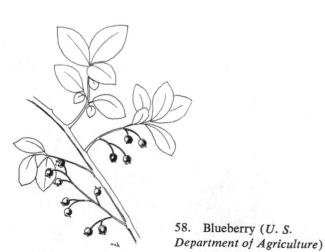

58. Blueberry (*U. S. Department of Agriculture*)

WHERE IT GROWS:    Species are found in most states. It prefers dry areas such as pine barrens and mountain slopes.

PART USED:    Ripe berries.

OTHER COLOR:    Gray.

## MORDANT

| | |
|---|---|
| Alum | 1 cup |
| Cream of tartar | ¼ cup |
| Water | 2 gallons |

Dissolve the alum and cream of tartar in the water. Bring to a boil, and add the wet wool. Boil gently for 1 hour. Hang up to dry.

## DYE BATH

| | |
|---|---|
| Blueberries | 1½ quarts |
| Copper sulfate | 2 tablespoons |
| Water | |

Crush the berries, cover with water, and soak for 1 hour. Then boil for 30 minutes. Strain, and discard the pulp. Add cold water to the liquid to make 2 gallons. Add the copper sulfate, and bring to a boil. Add the dampened, mordanted wool, and boil gently for 1 hour. Wash in soapy water and then rinse and dry.

## ELDERBERRY Sambucus canadensis L.

OTHER NAMES:    American elder, common elder, elder, sweet elder.

PLANT DESCRIPTION:    Shrubs growing to 12 feet in height, with bright white pith. The 5 to 11 leaflets per branch are elliptical to lance-shaped, bright green, sharply toothed, and smooth below. The fragrant white flowers grow in clusters up to 10 inches across. The fruit is ¼ inch across, usually purple, although some varieties have red, yellow, or green fruits.

59. Elderberry (*U. S. Department of Agriculture*)

WHERE IT GROWS: From Southeastern Canada, to Florida, Georgia, Texas, and Oklahoma. Its habitats include wet, damp, or rich soils, woods, roadsides, and fields.

PARTS USED: Berries, leaves.

OTHER COLORS: Yellow, purple.

## MORDANT

| | |
|---|---|
| Alum | ¾ cup |
| Cream of tartar | ¼ cup |
| Water | 2 gallons |

Dissolve the alum and cream of tartar in the water, and bring to a boil. Add the wet wool, and boil gently for 1 hour. Hang up to dry.

## DYE BATH

| | |
|---|---|
| Elderberries | 2 gallons |
| Salt | 1 tablespoon |
| Water | |

Crush the berries and boil with 1 gallon of water for 30 minutes. Strain, and discard the pulp. Add cold water to the liquid to make 2 gallons. Add the salt and bring to a boil. Add the dampened, mordanted wool, and boil gently for 30 minutes. Rinse and dry.

## HORSEBRIER *Smilax* spp.

OTHER NAMES:   Carrion-flower, catbrier, greenbrier.

PLANT DESCRIPTION:   A shrubby or climbing vine with some species growing to 16 feet in height, and there may be prickly stickers on the stem. The leaves are almost heart-shaped, up to 5 inches long toward the top of the plant, but may be shorter and narrow at the base. The tiny greenish or yellow flowers grow in umbels, later becoming small black berries.

60.   Horsebrier (*U. S. Forest Service*)

WHERE IT GROWS:   In the Eastern United States as far west as Kansas, south to Florida and Texas. In glades, open woods, ravines, low ground, stream bottoms, cultivated fields, meadows, waste places.

PART USED:   Ripe berries.

OTHER COLOR:   Purple.

## MORDANT

| | |
|---|---|
| Alum | ¾ cup |
| Cream of tartar | ¼ cup |
| Water | 2 gallons |

Dissolve the alum and cream of tartar in the water. Bring to a boil, and add the wet wool. Boil gently for 1 hour and 15 minutes. Hang up to dry.

## DYE BATH

| | |
|---|---|
| Horsebrier berries | 2 gallons |
| Salt | 2 cups |
| Water | |

Crush the berries, cover with water and boil for 1 hour. Strain, and discard the pulp. Add cold water to the liquid to make 2 gallons. Bring to a boil, and add the salt. Stir well, and add the dampened, mordanted wool. Boil gently for 35 minutes. Rinse and dry.

## INDIGO *Indigofera tinctoria* L.

OTHER NAME: Anil.

PLANT DESCRIPTION: An erect shrub growing to 6 feet in height. Leaves are compound with as many as 17 leaflets about 1½ inches long. Flowers are typical legumes, pink-purple, followed by legume-type pods, 1 inch and straight.

WHERE IT GROWS: Closely related species grow in the West from Kansas to northern Mexico; another is found in the Carolinas, Georgia, Alabama, Mississippi, Florida. The variety tinctoria is planted as a "living museum specimen" at Charles Towne Landing, Charleston, South Carolina.

PARTS USED: Aboveground parts after processing.

*Gouſſes de l'Anil*

*Anil*

61. Indigo
(*Smithsonian Institution, Division of Textiles, Rita Adrosko*)

## MORDANT

*METHOD 1*

None required.

## DYE BATH

*DYE A*

| | |
|---|---|
| powdered indigo | 4 ounces |
| hydrosulfite | 2½ ounces |
| sodium hydroxide (caustic soda) | 3 ounces |

*DYE B*

| | |
|---|---|
| powdered indigo | 2 ounces |
| hydrosulfite | 2 ounces |
| sodium hydroxide (caustic soda) | 3 ounces |

Measure 1 cup of warm water. Carefully and gently using rubber or plastic gloves, stir and dissolve the caustic soda. A rapid increase in water temperature will occur. DO NOT SPLASH ON HANDS OR FACE.

Using a large glass or enamel pot, measure 3 quarts of warm water and slowly add the hydrosulfite. Then make a thin paste of the indigo with a little warm water.

Using a battery-type hydrometer, check the caustic soda solution. It should give a reading of 1.175 to 2.0 specific gravity.

One-half cup of this solution is then added to the indigo paste. Then add 1 quart of the hydrosulfite solution to the indigo-caustic soda mix. The resulting stock solution will be a yellow color and is best stored in tightly stoppered bottles. Before using it, the amount to be used must be heated to about 120–30° F. and then left to stand for 1 hour.

For actual dyeing, an enamel pot of 3 to 4 gallons' capacity is needed. It should be filled with water to about 3 or 4 inches of the top and heated to 125° F.

To the warm water add 1 cup of the hydrosulfite solution.

The stock solution should be checked with a clear glass rod. If the dye stock on the rod is green turning to blue, it is ready for use.

If the rod shows irregular blue patches, add ½ cup of hydro-sulfite solution to the stock solution. If the glass rod has a milky white appearance, add ¼ cup of caustic solution.

One-third cup of the stock dye should be added gently to the water bath, and slowly warmed to 125° F.

The wetted wool is slowly stirred into the dye bath. After 5 to 10 minutes raise the wool out of the bath and observe the color. From green to a shade of blue is the process. Dyeing then is repeated until the desired blue is achieved. It may be necessary to add a tablespoon or two of dye stock. The temperature should be kept steady at 125–30° F.

When the color is satisfactory, the wool should be washed in a weak solution of a few drops of sulfuric acid in a gallon of water.

### METHOD 2

A shorter method for the indigo dyeing is available, requiring a sensitive paper used to measure caustic bath concentrations.

Three to 5 gallons of water are boiled in an enamel pot for about 1 hour, then cooled to 125° F. Slowly mix in caustic soda, using the sensitive paper until it turns to a color indicating a reading of 8 as shown on the color scale. Then measure ½ cup of indigo powder and make a paste with a little warm water and stir into the bath. Next stir in an equal amount of hydrosulfite and let set for 15 minutes. Bring the temperature to 125–30° F. Follow the procedure for Method 1.

A hot bath of some gentle soap after the acid bath is recommended for both dye methods.

## MORDANT

*METHOD 3*

| (For wool) | |
|---|---|
| Alum | 1 cup |
| Cream of tartar | ¼ cup |
| Water | 2 gallons |

Dissolve the alum and cream of tartar in the water. Bring to a boil, and add the wet wool. Boil gently for 1 hour. Hang up to dry.

| (For cotton) | |
|---|---|
| Alum | 1 cup |
| Washing soda | ¼ cup |
| Water | 2 gallons |

Dissolve the alum and washing soda in the water. Bring to a boil, and add the wet cotton. Boil gently for 1 hour. Let the cotton cool in the bath overnight. The next day hang up to dry.

## DYE BATH

This method, known as the blue-pot or fermentation vat, is the oldest method of dyeing with indigo, and depends on bacteria acting on the dye to reduce it to proper form. The color is lightened by using fewer dips in the dye bath, and darkened by increasing the number of dips, for wool or cotton.

For each pound of cotton or wool use:

8 ounces powdered indigo
4 ounces wheat bran
4 ounces madder
1½ pounds washing soda
4 gallons water

The dye ingredients are mixed and kept in a warm room for 50 to

100 days with daily stirring. When an unpleasant odor is obvious, and a blue scum forms on the surface, the dye pot is ready for use.

Before dipping the wool or cotton into the warmed dye pot (85° F.) wet the material thoroughly.

The material should be lifted out of the pot from time to time to develop blue color. This procedure should continue for 30 minutes, then squeeze out the dye and air for 20 to 30 minutes. Repeat this process, increasing dipping time until the desired color is achieved. To help get a uniform dye, the material is stirred gently from time to time.

Care should be used *not* to stir the sediment, to minimize streaking of the material. If the greenish color of the dye pot becomes blue from too much stirring, it must be replenished by adding the dye ingredients and allowing to stand 2 to 3 days.

## LARKSPUR *Delphinium* spp.

OTHER NAME:  Staggerweed.

PLANT DESCRIPTION:  An upright branching plant growing to 3 feet in height. The leaves are deeply lobed. The flowers may be blue, purple, or white, and are found at the top of the stem.

WHERE IT GROWS:  It is grown all over the United States in flower gardens, and also occurs in open, dry places as well as open woods, roadsides, and old fields.

PART USED:  Flowers.

### MORDANT

None required.

### DYE BATH

| | | |
|---|---|---|
| Larkspur flowers | 1½ gallons |
| Water | |
| Alum | ¾ cup |

Chop the flowers, cover with water, and boil for 40 minutes. Strain, and discard the flowers. Add cold water to the liquid to make 2 gallons. Bring to a boil, and add the alum. Add the wet, unmordanted wool, and boil gently for 30 to 40 minutes. Rinse and dry.

62. Larkspur (*University of West Virginia, from* FLORA OF WEST VIRGINIA)

## SORREL *Rumex* spp.

OTHER NAMES:  Cow sorrel, field sorrel, garden sorrel, horse sorrel, mountain sorrel, red sorrel, sour dock, sour-grass, toad sorrel.

PLANT DESCRIPTION:  One of several related sorrels and docks resembling each other. They have erect stems and lance-shaped leaves. The flowers range from yellow to purple and appear crowded on stalks at the top of the plant. The seeds are 3-sided nutlets, shiny brown or black. One species is grown for its edible leaves, *R. acetosa.*

63. Sorrel (Dock)
(*Colorado State
University, B. L.
Thornton and L. W.
Durrell, 1941.*
WEEDS OF COLORADO.
*Colorado Exp. Sta.
Bull. 466, Colorado
State College, Ft.
Collins*)

WHERE IT GROWS: Members of this group are found in Canada, and all states of the U.S., as well as Mexico, with habitats ranging from the deserts of Arizona and Mexico to swamps and marshes.

PARTS USED: Root, stalk, plant.

OTHER COLOR: Red.

## MORDANT

| | |
|---|---|
| Alum | 1 cup |
| Cream of tartar | ¼ cup |
| Water | 2 gallons |

Dissolve the alum and cream of tartar in the water. Bring to a boil, and add the wet wool. Boil gently for 30 minutes. Hang up to dry.

## DYE BATH

Sorrel plants    1½ gallons
Water

Chop the plants, cover with water, and soak overnight. The next day boil for 1 hour. Strain, and discard the plants. Add cold water to the liquid to make 2 gallons. Bring to a boil, and add the dampened, mordanted wool. Boil gently for 30 minutes. Rinse and dry.

# CHAPTER 10

# Purple dyes

## BLACK CHERRY *Prunus serotina* Ehrhart

OTHER NAMES:    Black choke, cabinet cherry, cherry, choke cherry, rum cherry, Virginia prince bark, whiskey cherry, wild black cherry.

PLANT DESCRIPTION:    A tree with dark, rough bark and reddish-brown branches, 4 to 5 feet in diameter, growing to a height of 100 feet. The inner bark is aromatic. The lance- to oval-shaped

64.    Black Cherry (*U. S. Forest Service*)

64a.    (*U. S. Forest Service*)

leaves are 2 to 6 inches long, toothed, and shiny above, smooth and lighter-colored below. The small white flowers grow in clusters 4 inches long. The thin-fleshed purplish-black cherries are ¼ inch or less in diameter, bitter but edible.

WHERE IT GROWS:   It grows from Canada, Minnesota, and North Dakota to Florida, west to Texas, and into Mexico. It is adapted to a wide range of habitats.

PARTS USED:   Bark, roots.

OTHER COLOR:   Brown.

## MORDANT

| | |
|---|---|
| Alum | ¾ cup |
| Cream of tartar | ¼ cup |
| Water | 2 gallons |

Dissolve the alum and cream of tartar in the water. Bring to a boil, and add the wet wool. Boil gently for 1 hour. Hang up to dry.

## DYE BATH

| | |
|---|---|
| Cherry roots | 1½ gallons |
| Water | |

Chop the roots, cover with water, and soak overnight. The next day boil for 1 hour. Strain, and discard the roots. Add cold water to the liquid to make 2 gallons. Bring to a boil, and add the dampened, mordanted wool. Boil gently for 1 hour. Rinse and dry.

## COCHINEAL *Coccus cacti* L. (an insect)

OTHER NAME:   Cochinolla.

DESCRIPTION:   Used by the Incas, Mayas, and Aztecs as a red dye, this louselike scale insect is fairly common. A similar insect has long been used in the Near East, collected from an oak tree.

WHERE IT IS FOUND:   It has long been harvested in Mexico, Honduras, Peru, and the Canary Islands, where it has been sometimes cultivated on a cactus on which it lives. The red dye comes from the females. When bloated with eggs they are scraped off the plant and killed in boiling water.

PARTS USED:   The cochineal of commerce is the mass of insect bodies dried in the sun or in an oven. Wide variation in quality and shade of red is common. The material can still be bought in the United States.

OTHER COLOR:   Red.

## MORDANT

Potassium dichromate     2 tablespoons
Water                    2 gallons

Dissolve the potassium dichromate in the water, and bring to a boil. Add the wet wool, and boil gently for 1 hour. Hang up to dry.

## DYE BATH

Cochineal, powdered     2½ ounces
Water                   2 gallons
Vinegar                 1 tablespoon

Combine the cochineal and vinegar with one quart of the water, and boil for 10 minutes. Strain, and discard the pulp. Add the remaining water to the liquid. Bring to a boil, and add the dampened, mordanted wool. Boil gently for 1½ hours. Rinse and dry.

## COCKLEBUR *Xanthium pensylvanicum* Wallr.

PLANT DESCRIPTION:   An erect, branching plant growing to 7 feet in height. The leaves are thick, slightly shiny, with very fine hairs. The familiar burs are green and scattered with stiff prickles. Many species are found and can be distinguished by botanists by the burs. *Xanthium* is the Greek word for yellow, so named because of its use to dye the hair golden.

WHERE IT GROWS:   It is common in Southern Canada and all

parts of the United States, in dry barren spots such as empty lots, abandoned fields and meadows.

PARTS USED:   Aboveground parts.

OTHER COLORS:   Brown, yellow.

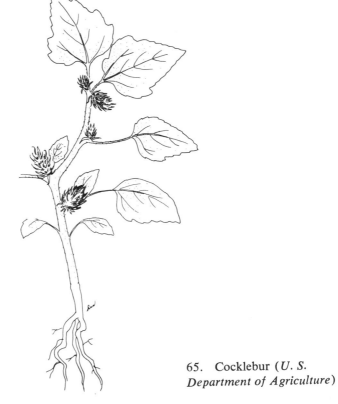

65.   Cocklebur (*U. S. Department of Agriculture*)

## MORDANT

None required.

## DYE BATH

| Cocklebur plants | 3 gallons |
|---|---|
| Alum | ¼ cup |
| Water | |

Chop the plants, cover with water, and boil for 2 hours. Strain, and discard the plants. Add cold water to the liquid to make 2 gallons. Bring to a boil, and add the alum. Stir well, and add the wet unmordanted wool. Boil gently for 30 minutes. Rinse and dry.

## DANDELION *Taraxacum officinale* Weber

OTHER NAMES: Blowball, cankerwort, doon-head-clock, milk witch, yellow gowan, witch's gowan.

PLANT DESCRIPTION: The all too familiar lance-shaped leaves with deep indentations grow close to the ground in the form of a rosette. The yellow flowers are 2 inches wide, and appear on hollow stalks that may grow to 1½ feet tall.

WHERE IT GROWS: In all parts of Canada and the United States, usually where it isn't wanted, generally lawns. It is found in drier areas such as meadows, empty lots, and pastures.

66.  Dandelion
(*U. S. Department of Agriculture*)

PART USED:   Roots.

OTHER COLOR:   Yellow.

## MORDANT

| | |
|---|---|
| Alum | 1 cup |
| Cream of tartar | ¼ cup |
| Water | 2 gallons |

Dissolve the alum and cream of tartar in the water. Bring to a boil, and add the wet wool. Boil gently for 1 hour. Hang up to dry.

## DYE BATH

| | |
|---|---|
| Dandelion roots | 2 quarts |
| Water | |

Chop the roots, cover with water, and soak overnight. The next day boil for 1 hour. Strain, and discard the roots. Add cold water to the liquid to make 2 gallons. Bring to a boil, and add the dampened, mordanted wool. Boil gently for 1 hour. Rinse and dry.

## ELDERBERRY *Sambucus canadensis* L.*

## MORDANT 1

| | |
|---|---|
| Alum | ½ cup |
| Cream of tartar | ¼ cup |
| Water | 2 gallons |

Dissolve the alum and cream of tartar in the water. Bring to a boil, and add the wet wool. Boil gently for 30 minutes. Hang up to dry.

## MORDANT 2

| | |
|---|---|
| Potassium dichromate | 2 tablespoons |
| Water | 2 gallons |

Dissolve the potassium dichromate in the water, and bring to a

* See Chapter 9 for plant description.

boil. Add the wet wool, and boil gently for 1 hour. Let cool in the water, and then hang up to dry.

## DYE BATH

Elderberries        2 gallons
Water

Crush the berries, cover with water, and boil for 30 minutes. Strain, and discard the pulp. Add cold water to the liquid to make 2 gallons. Add the dampened, mordanted wool, and boil gently for 30 minutes. Rinse and dry.

## GOOSEBERRY *Ribes* spp.

OTHER NAME:   Currant.

PLANT DESCRIPTION:   A great variety of shrubs growing to 12 feet in height with leaves that are usually lobed. The small white flowers grow singly or in small clusters. The globular fruits are found in almost any color, and many are used for food.

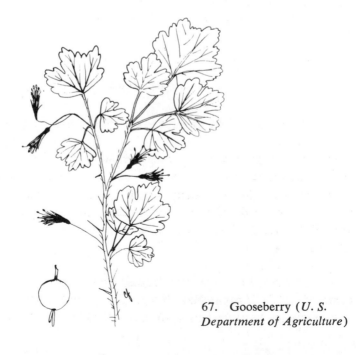

67.   Gooseberry (*U. S. Department of Agriculture*)

WHERE IT GROWS:   It is found across Canada as far south as Virginia and Texas, and elsewhere as a garden plant. In the wild the plants occur in drier and higher elevations.

PART USED:   Berries of the darker-fruited varieties.

## MORDANT

| | |
|---|---|
| Alum | ¼ cup |
| Cream of tartar | ¼ cup |
| Water | 2 gallons |

Dissolve the alum and cream of tartar in the water. Bring to a boil, and add the wet wool. Boil gently for 30 minutes. Hang up to dry.

## DYE BATH

| | |
|---|---|
| Gooseberries | 1½ quarts |
| Water | |

Crush the berries, cover with water, and soak overnight. The next day boil for 1 hour. Strain, and discard the pulp. Add cold water to the liquid to make 2 gallons. Bring to a boil, and add the dampened, mordanted wool. Boil gently for 30 minutes. Rinse and dry.

## GRAPE *Vitis* spp.

OTHER NAMES:   Fox grape, possum grape, vine, wild grape.

PLANT DESCRIPTION:   A very familar vine with small green inconspicuous flowers that grow in the characteristic pyramidal clusters later producing fruits, usually round or oblong, green, red, to black in color. The fruit of the wild varieties contain 3-sided seeds with very little pulp, while the cultivated varieties are more fleshy and luscious.

WHERE IT GROWS:   In the United States the cultivated areas are centered in California, New York, North and South Carolina. The wild varieties are abundant in most states but are most common from New England, west to Kansas, Wisconsin, Oklahoma, Colorado, south to Georgia, Florida, and Texas.

PART USED:   Ripe fruit of dark-colored varieties.

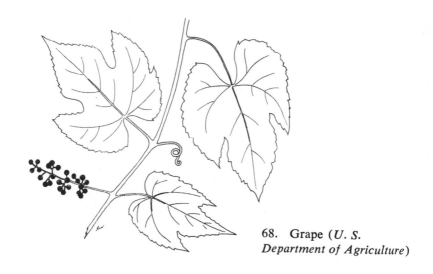

68.  Grape (*U. S.*
*Department of Agriculture*)

## MORDANT

| | |
|---|---|
| Alum | ½ cup |
| Cream of tartar | ¼ cup |
| Water | 2 gallons |

Dissolve the alum and cream of tartar in the water. Bring to a boil, and add the wet wool. Boil gently for 30 minutes. Hang up to dry.

## DYE BATH

| | |
|---|---|
| Grapes, ripe | 3 quarts |
| Water | |

Crush the grapes, cover with water and soak overnight. The next day boil for 1 hour. Strain and discard the pulp. Add cold water to the liquid to make 2 gallons. Bring to a boil, and add the dampened, mordanted wool. Boil gently for 1 hour. Rinse and dry.

## HORSEBRIER *Smilax* spp.*

### MORDANT

| | |
|---|---|
| Alum | 1 cup |
| Cream of tartar | ¼ cup |
| Water | 2 gallons |

Dissolve the alum and cream of tartar in the water. Bring to a boil, and add the wet wool. Boil gently for 1 hour and 15 minutes. Hang up to dry.

### DYE BATH

| | |
|---|---|
| Horsebrier berries | 2 gallons |
| Water | |

Crush the berries, cover with water, and boil for 1 hour. Strain, and discard the pulp. Add cold water to the liquid to make 2 gallons. Bring to a boil, and add the dampened, mordanted wool. Boil gently for 30 minutes. Rinse and dry.

## OAK *Quercus* spp.

OTHER NAMES:   Basket oak, black oak, live oak, pin water oak, post oak, Spanish oak, swamp oak, white oak.

PLANT DESCRIPTION:   A range of handsome trees much involved in legends, "Mighty oaks from little acorns grow" being one. The oak has been a symbol of strength and trueness. The flowers are catkins; the fruit acorns. There are over 20 major species in the United States.

WHERE IT GROWS:   Temperate climates and in some tropical highlands, usually in dry sunny areas.

PARTS USED:   Bark, extract, acorns.

OTHER COLORS:   Green, yellow, brown.

* See Chapter 9 for botanical information.

6. A house mask from New Guinea dyed with minerals and plants. *(Krochmal Collection of Primitive Art, D. H. Hill Library, North Carolina State University)*

7. and 8.   Dyeing and weaving are still carried on in Asia and the Middle East. In the top photo, Turkish dyers outside of Ankara rinse newly dyed materials in a convenient stream.

In the bottom photo, residents of the poor-house in Herat, Afghanistan, weave lovely rugs. *(Photo by the authors)*

9. The arts of dyeing and weaving flourish in modern Guatemala, and a commonly used color is a Latin version of Tyrian purple. With an antique-style loom, kneeling on a woven petate, this Indian woman weaves rugs and serapes. (*Dr. Carl E. Anderson, School of Medicine, University of North Carolina, Chapel Hill*)

10, 11, and 12.   An increasing interest in plants as dye sources has prompted the Great Smoky Mountains National Park, Gatlinburg, Tennessee, to schedule dye demonstrations. Ann Ragan displays the dyed wools here, and demonstrates the carding and spinning of wool and cotton. *(Great Smoky Mountains National Park)*

69. Oak (*Quercus lobata*) (*U. S. Forest Service*)

70. Oak (*Quercus nigra*) (*U. S. Forest Service*)

## MORDANT

None required.

## DYE BATH

Oak bark     3 gallons
Water

Chop the bark, cover with water, and boil for 2½ hours. Strain, and discard the bark. Add cold water to the liquid to make 2 gallons. Bring to a boil, and add the wet, unmordanted wool. Boil gently for 30 minutes. Rinse and dry.

## RED CEDAR *Juniperus virginiana* L.

OTHER NAMES: Carolina cedar, cedar, cedar apple, evergreen, green cedar, juniper, pencil cedar, red juniper, red savin, savin.

PLANT DESCRIPTION: An evergreen tree growing to 100 feet in height, varying in shape a great deal. Sometimes the bark is shreddy and tan or brown. The foliage is lightly aromatic and ranges in color from blue-green to pale green. The round blue-black waxy berries contain 1 to 3 seeds, and arise from female cones found on the tips of the branches.

WHERE IT GROWS:   The trees are distributed from Southeastern Canada as far south as Florida and to Missouri and Illinois. It grows best in dry open areas on poor soils.

PARTS USED:   Root, ripe berries.

OTHER COLOR:   Green.

## MORDANT

None required.

## DYE BATH

Red cedar root    1 gallon
Water

71.  Red Cedar (*U. S. Forest Service*)          71a.   (*U. S. Forest Service*)

Chop the root, cover with water, and soak for 2 hours. Then boil for 45 minutes. Strain, and discard the root. Add cold water to the liquid to make 2 gallons. Bring to a boil, and add the wet, unmordanted wool. Boil gently for 30 minutes. Rinse and dry.

# CHAPTER 11

# Red dyes

## BEDSTRAW *Galium aparine* L.

OTHER NAMES: Catchweed, cleavers, cling rascal, goose grass, grip grass, hedgeburr, scratch grass.

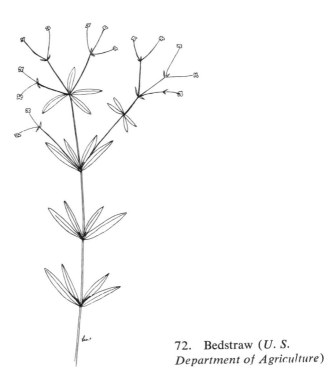

72. Bedstraw (*U. S. Department of Agriculture*)

PLANT DESCRIPTION: A sprawling, spreading plant with rough, many-branched square stems 2 to 5 feet in height. The hairy leaves, 1 to 2 inches long, grow in whorls; the small white or purplish flowers with 5 petals grow toward the top of the plant.

WHERE IT GROWS: It is widespread, growing from Alaska south through Canada to Florida and Texas. It appears most frequently in damp areas, such as woods, beaches, and forest areas.

PARTS USED: Roots, stalks.

OTHER COLOR: Orange.

## MORDANT

Alum     ¾ cup
Water    2 gallons

Dissolve the alum in the water and bring to a boil. Add the wet wool, and boil gently for 30 minutes. Hang up to dry.

## DYE BATH

Bedstraw roots    3 quarts
Water

Chop the roots, cover with water, and soak overnight. The next day boil for 2 hours. Strain, and discard the roots. Add cold water to the liquid to make 2 gallons. Bring to a boil, and add the dampened, mordanted wool. Boil gently for 25 minutes. Rinse and dry.

## BEETS *Beta vulgaris* L.

OTHER NAMES: Beetroot, mangels, sugar beets.

PLANT DESCRIPTION: This familar vegetable is available in the supermarket both fresh and canned. The reddish-green leaves, which resemble pokeberry leaves, are not used for dyeing.

PART USED: Roots.

OTHER COLORS: Yellow, brown.

73. Beets (*U. S. Department of Agriculture*)

## MORDANT

| | |
|---|---|
| Alum | 1 cup |
| Cream of tartar | ¼ cup |
| Water | 2 gallons |

Dissolve the alum and cream of tartar in the water. Bring to a boil, and add the wet wool. Boil gently for 30 minutes. Hang up to dry.

## DYE BATH

Beets, roots    1½ quarts (may be fresh or canned)
Water

Chop the beets, cover with water, and soak overnight. The next day boil for 1 hour. Strain, and discard the beets. Add cold water to the liquid to make 2 gallons. Bring to a boil, and add the dampened, mordanted wool. Boil gently for 1 hour. Rinse well and then wash in warm soapy water. Rinse again and dry.

## BLOODROOT *Sanguinaria canadensis* L.

OTHER NAMES: Puccoon, red Indian paint, red puccoon, red-root, turmeric.

PLANT DESCRIPTION: A forest plant with a thick root 2 to 6 inches long, orange-red in color. There is usually a single stalk 5 to 8 inches in height, topped by a single pale green leaf 6 to 12 inches wide and 4 to 6 inches long. The leaf is lobed to form 3 to 8 segments. The conspicuous flowers are generally white but may be purple to pink.

74. Bloodroot (*U. S. Department of Agriculture*)

WHERE IT GROWS: It grows in Southern Canada, New England to Kentucky and Florida, west to Kansas and Nebraska, in damp, heavily wooded areas.

PART USED: Roots.

OTHER COLOR: Yellow.

## MORDANT

None required.

## DYE BATH

| | |
|---|---|
| Bloodroot roots | 3 quarts |
| Oak bark | 1 cup |
| Water | |

Chop the roots and bark, cover with water, and soak overnight. The next day boil for 1 hour. Strain, and discard the plant materials. Add cold water to the liquid to make 2 gallons. Bring to a boil, and add the wet, unmordanted wool. Boil gently for 50 minutes. Rinse and dry.

## CARDINAL FLOWER *Lobelia cardinalis* L.

OTHER NAMES: Cardinal lobelia, highbelia, hog-physic, Indian pink, red cardinal, red lobelia.

PLANT DESCRIPTION: A tall and graceful plant growing from 2 to 4 feet in height, smooth and unbranched. The leaves are toothed and smooth. The flowers are usually bright red, but sometimes white, and grow at the top of the stem.

WHERE IT GROWS: It is found in Southern and Eastern Canada, south to Florida, west to Texas, and in the Midwest, usually along streams and in damp, shady areas.

PART USED: Flowers.

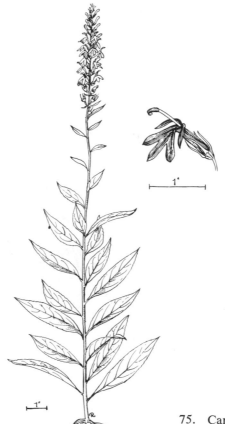

75. Cardinal Flower (*U. S. Forest Service*)

## MORDANT

Alum     1 cup
Water    2 gallons

Dissolve the alum in the water, and bring to a boil. Add the wet wool and boil gently for 1½ hours. Let the wool cool in the water, and then hang up to dry.

## DYE BATH

Cardinal flowers, fresh     2 to 3 quarts
Water

Cover the flowers with water, and boil for 20 minutes. Strain, and discard the flowers. Add cold water to the liquid to make 2 gallons. Bring to a boil, and add the dampened, mordanted wool. Boil gently for 45 minutes. Rinse and dry.

## COCHINEAL *Coccus cacti* L.*

### MORDANT

*METHOD 1*

| Muriate of tin | 2 tablespoons |
| Cream of tartar | 3 tablespoons |
| Water | 2 gallons |

Dissolve the muriate of tin and cream of tartar in the water. Bring to a boil, and add the wet wool. Boil gently for 2 hours. Hang up to dry.

### DYE BATH

| Cochineal, powdered | 2 ounces |
| Water | 2 gallons |

Bring the water to a boil, and add the cochineal. Stir well, and add the dampened, mordanted wool. Boil gently for 1 hour. Rinse and dry.

### MORDANT

*METHOD 2*

| Alum | 1 cup |
| Cream of tartar | ¼ cup |
| Water | 2 gallons |

Dissolve the alum and cream of tartar in the water. Bring to a boil, and add the wet wool. Boil gently for 1 hour. Hang up to dry.

### DYE BATH

| Cochineal | 1 ounce |
| Water | |

* See Chapter 10 for scientific information.

Soak the cochineal in 1 pint of water for 1 hour. Add 1 gallon of water, and boil for 30 minutes. Strain, and add cold water to make 2 gallons. Bring to a boil, and add the dampened, mordanted wool. Boil gently for 1 hour. Rinse and dry.

The mordant and dye bath can be combined into one step by adding the alum and cream of tartar to the dye bath just before adding the wet wool.

## MORDANT

*METHOD 3*

None required.

## DYE BATH

| | |
|---|---|
| Cochineal | 1 ounce |
| Oxalic acid | ¾ cup |
| Stannous chloride | 1 cup |
| Cream of tartar | ¼ cup |

Soak the cochineal overnight in 1 pint of water. The next day add the oxalic acid, stannous chloride, and cream of tartar, and boil for 10 minutes. Add cold water to make 2 gallons, and then bring to a boil. Add the wet wool, and boil gently for 1 hour. Rinse and dry.

## COREOPSIS *Coreopsis* spp.

PLANT DESCRIPTION: A plant growing to 10 feet in height with a smooth stem and deeply lobed leaves. The yellow flowers have notched petals.

WHERE IT GROWS: Different species are found growing in all parts of the United States in almost all kinds of sites from open prairies to forests.

PARTS USED: Blossoms, leaves, stalks.

OTHER COLOR: Yellow.

76. Coreopsis (*U. S.
Department of Agriculture*)

## MORDANT

| | |
|---|---|
| Potassium dichromate | ½ cup |
| Water | 2 gallons |

Dissolve the potassium dichromate in the water. Bring to a boil, and add the wet wool. Boil gently for 1 hour. Hang up to dry.

## DYE BATH

| | |
|---|---|
| Coreopsis flowers | 1½ quarts |
| Water | |

Chop the flowers, cover with water, and soak overnight. The next day boil for 25 minutes. Strain, and discard the flowers. Add cold water to the liquid to make 2 gallons. Bring to a boil, and add the dampened, mordanted wool. Boil gently for 25 minutes. Rinse and dry.

## DOGWOOD *Cornus* spp.

OTHER NAMES: Bunchberry, cornel, crackerberry, osier, pudding berry, red willow.

PLANT DESCRIPTION: A number of closely related trees or shrubs bearing white or greenish white flowers in a familiar 4-petal shape, giving rise to bright red berries much enjoyed by birds and other wildlife.

WHERE IT GROWS: Members of this group are found from Alaska to New Mexico, and Arizona, Texas, and Oklahoma, east to New England, and Florida.

PART USED: Roots.

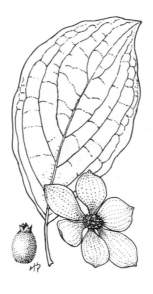

77. Dogwood (*U. S. Forest Service*)

## MORDANT

None required.

## DYE BATH

Dogwood root bark 1 gallon
Water

Chop the root bark, cover with water, and soak overnight. The next day boil for 1 hour. Strain, and discard the bark. Add cold water to the liquid to make 2 gallons. Bring to a boil, and add the wet, unmordanted wool. Boil gently for 1 hour. Rinse and dry.

## HOLLYHOCK *Althaea rosea* Cav.

PLANT DESCRIPTION:   A tall leafy stemmed plant growing to 9 feet in height. The large rough leaves, growing from long stalks, are rounded to heart-shaped, with 5 to 7 lobes. The various colored flowers are 3 inches across.

78.  Hollyhock (*University of West Virginia, from* FLORA OF WEST VIRGINIA)

WHERE IT GROWS:   It is common in flower gardens, roadsides, trash heaps, and empty lots, all over the United States.

PARTS USED:   Leaves, flowers.

OTHER COLOR:   Green.

### MORDANT

| | |
|---|---|
| Alum | ½ cup |
| Cream of tartar | ¼ cup |
| Water | 2 gallons |

Dissolve the alum and cream of tartar in the water. Bring to a boil, and add the wet wool. Boil gently for 30 minutes. Hang up to dry.

## DYE BATH

Hollyhock flowers, red, fresh      2 quarts
Water

Chop the flowers, cover with water, and soak for 4 hours. Boil for 1 hour, and strain. Discard the flowers, and add cold water to the liquid to make 2 gallons. Bring to a boil, and add the dampened, mordanted wool. Boil gently for 30 minutes. Rinse and dry.

## MADDER *Rubia tinctorium* L.

PLANT DESCRIPTION: A climbing plant with lance-shaped leaves 2 to 4 inches long with short or no leaf stalks. Flowers are borne in clusters at the top of the stalks. The long red roots were the major dye of medieval Europe.

Garance.

79. Madder (*Smithsonian Institution, Division of Textiles, Rita Adrosko*)

WHERE IT GROWS: It has been planted much in Europe; it is found also in the Mediterranean countries and Africa, Asia, and cool South American areas.

PART USED: Roots.

OTHER COLOR: Orange.

## MORDANT

*METHOD 1*

| | |
|---|---|
| Alum | ¼ cup |
| Water | 2 gallons |

Dissolve the alum in the water and bring to a boil. Add the wet wool, and boil gently for 1 hour. Hang up to dry.

## DYE BATH

| | |
|---|---|
| Madder | 2 ounces |
| Water | |

Soak the madder overnight in 1 quart of water. The next day add cold water to make 2 gallons, and bring to a boil. Add the dampened, mordanted wool. Boil gently for 30 minutes. Rinse and dry. The next day wash in warm soapy water. Then rinse and dry.

## MORDANT 1

*METHOD 2*

| | |
|---|---|
| Potassium dichromate | 2 tablespoons |
| Water | 2 gallons |

Dissolve the potassium dichromate in the water. Bring to a boil, and add the wet wool. Boil gently for 1 hour. Hang up to dry.

## MORDANT 2

| | |
|---|---|
| Alum | 1 cup |
| Cream of tartar | ¼ cup |
| Water | 2 gallons |

Dissolve the alum and cream of tartar in the water. Bring to a boil, and add the wet wool. Boil gently for 1 hour. Hang up to dry.

## MORDANT 3

Muriate of tin    ¼ cup plus 2 tablespoons
Cream of tartar   ¾ cup plus 2 tablespoons
Water             2 gallons

Dissolve the muriate of tin and cream of tartar in the water. Bring to a boil, and add the wet wool. Boil gently for 2 hours. Hang up to dry.

## DYE BATH

Madder   ½ to 1 pound
Water

Soak the madder overnight in 1 gallon of water. The next day add water to make 2 gallons and bring to a boil. Add the dampened, mordanted wool. Boil gently for 1½ hours. Let the wool cool in the water, and then rinse and dry.

## MORDANT

*METHOD 3*

(For cotton only)
Alum           2 cups
Washing soda   ½ cup
Tannic acid    2 tablespoons
Water

Dissolve 1 cup of alum and ¼ cup of the washing soda in 2 gallons of water. Add the wet cotton, and bring to a boil. Boil gently for 1 hour. Let the cotton cool in the bath overnight.

The next day bring 2 gallons of water to a boil and add the tannic acid. Remove the cotton from the water that it has been sitting in; squeeze gently and add to the hot bath containing the tannic acid. Boil gently for 1 hour, stirring frequently. Let the cotton remain in this overnight.

The next day dissolve the remaining cup of alum and ¼ cup of washing soda in 2 gallons of hot water. Remove the cotton from the bath it has been sitting in and rinse. Add the cotton to the bath containing the alum and washing soda, and boil gently for 1 hour, stirring occasionally. Let the cotton remain in the bath overnight.

The next day squeeze the cotton out and hang up to dry.

## DYE BATH

Madder    8 ounces
Water

Soak 2 ounces of madder overnight in 1 quart of water. The next day add cold water to make 2 gallons. Bring to a boil, and add the dampened, mordanted cotton. Boil gently for 1 hour. Leave the cotton in this dye bath overnight. Soak 3 ounces more of madder in 1 quart of water overnight.

The next day repeat the dye bath, using the madder soaked the night before to replace the old dye bath. Soak the remaining 3 ounces of madder for use the next day.

The next day repeat the dye bath again. Remove the cotton from the dye bath and rinse and dry.

## POKEBERRY *Phytolacca americana* L.

OTHER NAMES:   American cancer, cancer jalap, coakum, garget, ink-berry, pigeonberry, pocom-bush, pokeweed, red-ink plant, red-weed.

80. Pokeberry
(*U. S. Department of Agriculture*)

PLANT DESCRIPTION: A shrub with purplish, smooth, heavy, branching stems growing 3 to 12 feet in height. The thick, smooth, elliptical leaves are 6 to 12 inches long, green above and purple beneath. The small white flowers grow in separate stalks. The fruits are purple, and grow in clusters in great numbers. The roots are very thick. The tops die back over winter.

WHERE IT GROWS: Southeastern Canada, New England south to Florida and Texas are the range of this vigorous plant. It appears as a dynamic invader on newly cleared areas, on strip-mined locations, empty fields, and fence rows.

PART USED: Berries.

## MORDANT

| Vinegar | ½ gallon |
| Water | 1½ gallons |

Combine the vinegar and water, and bring to a boil. Add the wet wool, and boil gently for 1 hour. Hang up to dry.

## DYE BATH 1

| Pokeberry fruit juice | 2 gallons |
| Vinegar | 1 gallon |

Combine the juice and vinegar, and bring to a boil. Add the dampened, mordanted wool, and boil gently for 1 hour. Hang up to dry without rinsing. When dry, wash in warm soapy water, and rinse well. Hang up to dry.

## DYE BATH 2

| Pokeberries | 3 gallons |
| Vinegar | 1 gallon |
| Water | |

Combine the berries, vinegar, and ½ gallon of water. Boil for 40 minutes. Strain, and discard the pulp. Add cold water to the liquid to make 2 gallons. Bring to a boil, and add the dampened, mordanted wool. Boil gently for 45 minutes. Hang up to dry without rinsing. Then rinse and dry.

## POPPY *Papaver* spp.

OTHER NAMES:   Amapola, canker rose, redweed.

PLANT DESCRIPTION:   The flowers are large, showy and occur singly on a long stem. The plants produce a milky sap. The most noted is the opium poppy, *P. somniferum,* "the sleepy poppy."

WHERE IT GROWS:   A favorite garden plant, the poppy grows almost anywhere.

PART USED:   Red flowers.

81.   Poppy (*University of West Virginia, from* FLORA OF WEST VIRGINIA)

## MORDANT

Alum     1 cup
Water     2 gallons

Dissolve the alum in the water, and bring to a boil. Add the wet wool, and boil gently for 1 hour. Hang up to dry.

## DYE BATH

Poppy flowers, red     ½ gallon
Water

Chop the flowers, cover with water, and boil for 45 minutes.

Strain, and discard the flowers. Add cold water to the liquid to make 2 gallons. Bring to a boil, and add the dampened, mordanted wool. Boil gently for 25 minutes. Rinse and dry.

## ST. JOHN'S WORT *Hypericum* spp.

OTHER NAMES: Herb of St. John's, orange grass, nits and lice, pineweed, speckled John.

PLANT DESCRIPTION: An erect plant or shrub growing to 6 feet in height. Flowers have 5 petals, and vary from orange, yellow, flesh to purple. A great many variations in leaves, flowers, and bark are found, making a generalized description difficult.

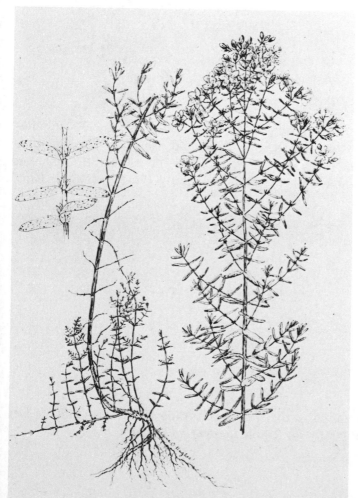

82. St. John's Wort (*U. S. Department of Agriculture*)

WHERE IT GROWS: Species grow in Canada and the Eastern and Midwest states as far west as Texas, Minnesota, Nebraska, Kansas, Colorado, North Dakota, and Washington, and south to Florida, Georgia, Alabama, and Louisiana. It is found under a wide range of conditions.

PARTS USED: Flowers, leaves.

OTHER COLOR: Yellow.

## MORDANT

None required.

## DYE BATH

| | |
|---|---|
| St. John's wort leaves | 3 quarts |
| Alum | ¾ cup |
| Water | |

Crush the leaves, cover with water, and boil for 35 minutes. Strain, and discard the leaves. Add cold water to the liquid to make 2 gallons. Bring to a boil, and add the alum. Stir well, and add the wet, unmordanted wool. Boil gently for 50 minutes. Rinse and dry.

## SORREL *Rumex* spp.*

## MORDANT

| | |
|---|---|
| Alum | 1 cup |
| Water | 2 gallons |

Dissolve the alum in the water, and bring to a boil. Add the wet wool, and boil gently for 2 hours. Hang up to dry.

* See Chapter 9 for botanical information.

## DYE BATH

Sorrel stalks, roots      3 gallons
Water

Chop the roots and stalks, cover with water, and soak overnight. The next day boil for 1 hour. Strain, and discard the plant material. Add cold water to the liquid to make 2 gallons. Bring to a boil, and add the dampened, mordanted wool. Boil gently for 30 minutes. Rinse and dry.

# CHAPTER 12

# Brown dyes

## ALDER *Alnus* spp.*

**Brown** MORDANT

*METHOD 1*

| | |
|---|---|
| Alum | ½ cup |
| Cream of tartar | ¼ cup |
| Water | 2 gallons |

Dissolve the alum and cream of tartar in the water. Bring to a boil, and add the wet wool. Boil gently for 30 minutes. Hang up to dry. If alder roots are used, increase the alum to 1 cup.

### DYE BATH

| | |
|---|---|
| Alder bark or roots | 1 gallon |
| Water | |

Chop the bark or roots, cover with water, and soak overnight. The next day boil for 1½ hours. Strain, and discard the plant material. Add cold water to the liquid to make 2 gallons. Bring to a boil, and add the dampened, mordanted wool. Boil gently for 1 hour. Rinse and dry.

* See Chapter 13 for botanical information.

## MORDANT

None required.

## DYE BATH

Alder bark      1 gallon
Water

Chop the bark, cover with water, and soak overnight. The next day boil for 1 hour. Strain, and discard the bark. Add cold water to the liquid to make 2 gallons. Bring to a boil, and add the dampened, unmordanted wool. Boil gently for 2 hours. Let cool in the dye bath. Then rinse and dry.

## APPLE *Malus* spp.

PLANT DESCRIPTION:   Apple trees are familiar to all. The trees are usually found in rows, but in Kentucky, Tennessee, and North Carolina we have often found old gnarled trees in the forests, near homesites abandoned decades ago, but still living vigorously and producing aromatic if small crops of fruits.

WHERE IT GROWS:   Wherever man settles in temperate zones, and in high elevations in Central America.

PART USED:   Bark.

OTHER COLOR:   Yellow.

**Yellow-brown**              MORDANT

Alum                1 cup
Cream of tartar     ¼ cup
Water               2 gallons

Dissolve the alum and cream of tartar in the water. Bring to a boil, and add the wet wool. Boil gently for 1 hour. Hang up to dry.

## DYE BATH

Apple bark    2½ gallons
Water

Chop the bark, cover with water, and soak overnight. The next day boil for 2 hours. Strain, and discard the bark. Add cold water to the liquid to make 2 gallons. Bring to a boil, and add the dampened, mordanted wool. Boil gently for 30 minutes. Rinse and dry. (The mordant can be eliminated and ¼ cup of alum can be added to the dye bath just before adding the wet wool.)

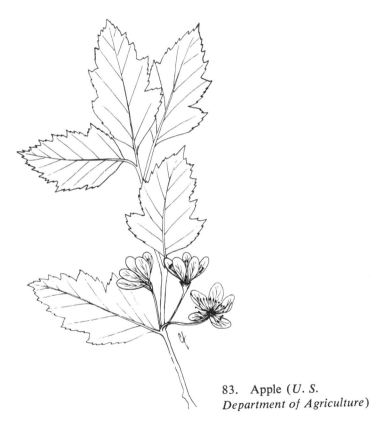

83.  Apple (*U. S. Department of Agriculture*)

## BAYBERRY *Myrica cerifera* L.

OTHER NAMES: American vegetable tallow, bayberry tallow, bearing myrica, candleberry, myrtle tree, puckerbush, southern wax myrtle, wax myrtle.

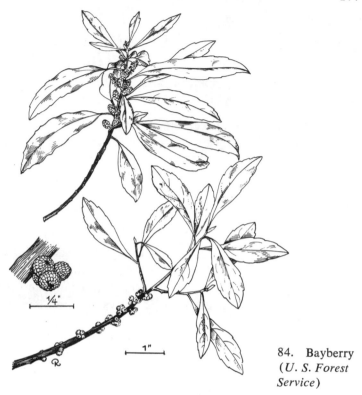

84. Bayberry
(*U. S. Forest
Service*)

PLANT DESCRIPTION: A small aromatic tree or shrub growing to 35 feet in height, with a trunk diameter of 6 to 8 inches. The leaves are lance-shaped, finely toothed, 1 to 3 inches long, somewhat sticky on both sides. The fruits are round, white or blue, and smaller than a blueberry. This most interesting plant has the ability to fix nitrogen from the air and inside the soil, although not a legume.

WHERE IT GROWS: It is found from New Jersey south to Florida, Alabama, Georgia, Mississippi, and Texas. It grows along coastal areas and banks of streams, in pine barrens, and mixed forests.

PART USED: Leaves.

OTHER COLOR: Yellow.

**Tan**

### MORDANT

| | |
|---|---|
| Alum | ¾ cup |
| Cream of tartar | ¼ cup |
| Water | 2 gallons |

Dissolve the alum and cream of tartar in the water. Bring to a boil, and add the wet wool. Boil gently for 45 minutes. Hang up to dry.

### DYE BATH

| | |
|---|---|
| Bayberry leaves | 1¾ gallons |
| Water | |

Chop the leaves, cover with water, and soak overnight. The next day boil for 1½ hours. Strain, and discard the leaves. Add cold water to the liquid to make 2 gallons. Bring to a boil, and add the dampened, mordanted wool. Boil gently for 45 minutes. Rinse and dry.

## BEECH *Fagus* spp.

OTHER NAME:   European beech.

PLANT DESCRIPTION:   A tree growing to 100 feet in height, with smooth light gray bark and light green toothed leaves. The fruit has prickles.

WHERE IT GROWS:   New England west to the Great Lakes states, and south to Ohio, Indiana, Illinois, and Missouri, Texas, and Florida. It prefers moist rich areas at higher elevations.

PARTS USED:   Leaves, fresh or dried, bark.

**Light tan**

### MORDANT

*METHOD 1*

| | |
|---|---|
| Alum | 1 cup |
| Cream of tartar | ¼ cup |
| Water | 2 gallons |

85. Beech (*U. S. Forest Service*)

Dissolve the alum and cream of tartar in the water. Bring to a boil, and add the wet wool. Boil gently for 1 hour. Hang up to dry.

### DYE BATH

| | |
|---|---|
| Beech leaves, fresh or dried | 2 gallons |
| Water | |

Chop the leaves, cover with water, and soak overnight. The next day boil for 50 minutes. Strain, and discard the leaves. Add cold water to the liquid to make 2 gallons. Bring to a boil, and add the dampened, mordanted wool. Boil gently for 30 minutes. Rinse and dry.

**Dark tan**              MORDANT

*METHOD 2*

| | |
|---|---|
| Oxalic acid | ¼ cup |
| Copperas | 3 tablespoons |
| Water | 2 gallons |

Dissolve the oxalic acid and copperas in the water. Bring to a boil, and add the wet wool. Boil gently for 1½ hours. Hang up to dry.

## DYE BATH

Beech bark  1 gallon
Water

Chop the bark, cover with water, and soak overnight. The next day boil for 1 hour. Strain, and discard the bark. Add cold water to the liquid to make 2 gallons. Bring to a boil, and add the dampened, mordanted wool. Boil gently for 45 minutes. Rinse and dry.

## BEETS *Beta vulgaris* L.*

**Rust brown**

### MORDANT

Alum  ¼ cup
Cream of tartar  ¼ cup
Water  2 gallons

Dissolve the alum and cream of tartar in the water. Bring to a boil, and add the wet wool. Boil gently for 30 minutes. Hang up to dry.

### DYE BATH

Beets  1½ quarts
Water

Chop the beets, cover with water, and boil for 1 hour. If canned beets are used, just add the liquid in the can to the water. Strain, and discard the beets. Add cold water to the liquid to make 2 gallons. Add mordanted wool. Boil gently for 1 hour. Rinse and dry.

## BIRCH *Betula* spp.

PLANT DESCRIPTION: A tree or shrub, growing to 100 feet in height, with smooth bark, separating in sheets. The leaves are usually heart- or wedge-shaped, sometimes toothed. The most famous is the paper birch.

WHERE IT GROWS: All through Canada, Alaska, Washington, to the Eastern states and south to Georgia. It prefers moist lowlands, and is often found near streams.

* See Chapter 11 for botanical information.

86. Birch (*U. S. Forest Service*)

PARTS USED: Bark, leaves.

OTHER COLOR: Yellow.

**Gray-brown**

### MORDANT

| | |
|---|---|
| Alum | 1 cup |
| Cream of tartar | ¼ cup |
| Water | 2 gallons |

Dissolve the alum and cream of tartar in the water. Bring to a boil, and add the wet wool. Boil gently for 1 hour. Hang up to dry.

### DYE BATH

| | |
|---|---|
| Birch leaves, dry | 2½ gallons (or 1 gallon birch bark) |
| Water | |

Crush the leaves or bark, cover with water, and soak overnight. The next day boil for 1 hour. Strain, and discard the leaves or bark. Add cold water to the liquid to make 2 gallons. Bring to a boil, and add the dampened, mordanted wool. Boil gently for 30 minutes. Rinse and dry.

## BLACK CHERRY *Prunus serotina* Ehrhart*

**Tan**                    MORDANT

Alum     ¼ cup
Water    2 gallons

Dissolve the alum in the water, and bring to a boil. Add the wet wool, and boil gently for 1 hour. Hang up to dry.

### DYE BATH

Black cherry bark     2 gallons
Water

Chop the bark, cover with water, and soak overnight. The next day boil for 1 hour. Strain, and discard the bark. Add cold water to the liquid to make 2 gallons. Bring to a boil, and add the dampened, mordanted wool. Boil gently for 30 minutes. Rinse and dry.

## BLACK WALNUT *Juglans nigra* L.**

**Dark brown**              MORDANT

*METHOD 1*

None required.

### DYE BATH

Black walnut leaves     2 gallons
Water

Layer the wool and the leaves in a pot. Cover with water and seal the pot. Let set for a week, and then remove the wool, rinse, and dry.

* See Chapter 10 for botanical information.
** See Chapter 13 for botanical information.

**Light brown**  MORDANT

*METHOD 2*

None required.

### DYE BATH

(For wool or cotton)
Walnut hulls, dry  2½ gallons
Water

Cover the hulls with water and soak for 1 hour. Then boil for 1 hour, and strain. Discard the hulls. Add cold water to the liquid to make 2 gallons. Bring to a boil, and add the wet, unmordanted cotton or wool. Boil gently for 30 minutes. Rinse and dry.

### MORDANT

*METHOD 3*

Alum  1 cup
Cream of tartar  ¼ cup
Water  2 gallons

Dissolve the alum and cream of tartar in the water. Bring to a boil, and add the wet wool. Boil gently for 1 hour. Hang up to dry.

**Dark brown**  DYE BATH 1

Walnut hulls, dry  ½ gallon
Water

Cover the hulls with water, and soak for 2 hours. Boil for 1 hour, and strain. Discard the hulls and add cold water to the liquid to make 2 gallons. Bring to a boil, and add the dampened, mordanted wool. Boil gently for 30 minutes. Transfer to a bath containing:

Potassium dichromate  1½ teaspoons
Vinegar  ⅓ cup
Water, boiling  2 gallons

Boil gently for 10 minutes. Rinse and dry. (If desired, the mordant can be eliminated as well as the afterbath.)

**Light brown**                DYE BATH 2

> Walnut bark       2 gallons
> Water

Chop the bark, cover with water, and soak overnight. The next day boil for 1½ hours. Strain, and discard the bark. Add cold water to the liquid to make 2 gallons. Bring to a boil, and add the dampened, mordanted wool. Boil gently for 30 minutes. Transfer to a bath containing:

> Potassium dichromate or copper sulfate    1½ teaspoons
> Vinegar                                    ⅓ cup
> Water, boiling                             2 gallons

Boil gently for 10 minutes. Rinse and dry.


**Medium brown**              MORDANT

*METHOD 4*

None required.


DYE BATH

> Walnut hulls      2 gallons
> Sumac berries     1½ cups
> Copperas          1 teaspoon
> Water

Cover the hulls with water, and boil for 30 minutes. Add the sumac berries, and boil for 40 minutes longer. Strain, and discard the hulls and sumac berries. Add cold water to the liquid to make 2 gallons. Bring to a boil and add the copperas. Stir well, and add the wet unmordanted wool. Boil gently for 45 minutes. Let the wool cool in the bath overnight. The next day rinse and dry.

## BUTTERNUT *Juglans cinerea* L.*

**Brown**                    MORDANT

|                  |            |
|------------------|------------|
| Alum             | 1 cup      |
| Cream of tartar  | ¼ cup      |
| Water            | 2 gallons  |

Dissolve the alum and cream of tartar in the water. Bring to a boil, and add the wet wool. Boil gently for 1 hour. Hang up to dry.

### DYE BATH 1

|                                  |             |
|----------------------------------|-------------|
| Butternut hulls, fresh or dried  | 1½ gallons  |
| Water                            |             |

Cover the hulls with water and soak overnight. The next day boil for 1 hour. Strain, and discard the hulls. Add cold water to the liquid to make 2 gallons. Bring to a boil, and add the dampened, mordanted wool. Boil gently for 30 minutes. Rinse and dry. If desired the mordant can be eliminated.

### DYE BATH 2

|                        |            |
|------------------------|------------|
| Butternut hulls, green | 2 gallons  |
| Water                  |            |

Cover the hulls with water, and soak for 30 minutes. Boil for 40 minutes, and strain. Discard the hulls, and add cold water to the liquid to make 2 gallons. Bring to a boil, and add the dampened, mordanted wool. Boil gently for 30 minutes. Transfer to a bath containing:

|                |                |
|----------------|----------------|
| Copperas       | 1½ teaspoons   |
| Water, boiling | 2 gallons      |

Boil gently for 10 minutes. Rinse and dry.

* See Chapter 14 for botanical information.

## CAMOMILE *Anthemis* spp.*

**Yellow-tan**

### MORDANT

| | |
|---|---|
| Alum | 1 cup |
| Cream of tartar | ¼ cup |
| Water | 2 gallons |

Dissolve the alum and cream of tartar in the water. Bring to a boil, and add the wet wool. Boil gently for 1 hour. Hang up to dry.

### DYE BATH

| | |
|---|---|
| Camomile flowers, yellow | 1¾ gallons |
| Water | |

Crush the flowers, cover with water, and boil for 40 minutes. Strain, and discard the flowers. Add cold water to the liquid to make 2 gallons. Bring to a boil, and add the dampened, mordanted wool. Boil gently for 30 minutes. Rinse and dry.

## CHITTIM *Rhamnus* spp.**

### MORDANT

| | |
|---|---|
| (For wool) | |
| Alum | 1 cup |
| Cream of tartar | ¼ cup |
| Water | 2 gallons |

Dissolve the alum and cream of tartar in the water. Bring to a boil, and add the wet wool. Boil gently for 1 hour. Hang up to dry.

* See Chapter 8 for botanical information.
** See Chapter 14 for botanical information.

(For cotton)
Alum                  2 cups
Washing soda          ½ cup
Tannic acid           2 tablespoons
Water

Dissolve 1 cup of the alum and ¼ cup of the washing soda in 2 gallons of water. Add the wet cotton, and bring to a boil. Boil gently for 1 hour. Let the cotton cool in the bath overnight.

The next day bring 2 gallons of water to a boil and add the tannic acid. Remove the cotton from the water that it has been sitting in, squeeze gently, and add to the hot bath containing the tannic acid. Boil gently for 1 hour, stirring frequently. Let the cotton remain in this overnight.

The next day dissolve the remaining cup of alum and ¼ cup of washing soda in 2 gallons of hot water. Remove the cotton from the water it has been sitting in and rinse. Add the cotton to the bath containing the alum and washing soda, and boil gently for 1 hour, stirring occasionally. Let the cotton remain in the bath overnight.

The next day squeeze the cotton out and hang up to dry.


**Dark tan**                    DYE BATH 1


Chittim bark          2½ quarts
Water


Chop the bark, cover with water, and soak overnight. The next day boil for 2 hours. Strain, and discard the bark. Add cold water to the liquid to make 2 gallons. Bring to a boil, and add the dampened, mordanted wool or cotton. Boil gently for 30 minutes. For cotton, transfer to a bath containing:


Potassium dichromate     1½ teaspoons
Vinegar                  ⅓ cup
Water, boiling           2 gallons


Boil gently for 10 minutes. Rinse and dry.

**Yellow-brown**                    DYE BATH 2

| Persian berry extract | 2 tablespoons |
| Water | 2 gallons |

Dissolve the extract in the water. Bring to a boil, and add the dampened, mordanted wool or cotton. Boil gently for 30 minutes. Transfer to a bath containing:

| Potassium dichromate | 1½ teaspoons |
| Vinegar | ⅓ cup |
| Water, boiling | 2 gallons |

Boil gently for 10 minutes. Rinse and dry.

## COCKLEBUR *Xanthium pensylvanicum* Wallr.*

**Light tan**                    MORDANT

None required.

### DYE BATH

| Cocklebur plants | 3 gallons |
| Water | |
| Alum | 1 teaspoon |

Cover the plants with water, and boil for 2 hours. Strain, and discard the plants. Add cold water to the liquid to make 2 gallons. Bring to a boil, and add the alum. Stir well, and add the wet, unmordanted wool. Boil gently for 30 minutes. Rinse and dry.

## COFFEE *Coffea arabica* L.

OTHER NAMES:   Arabian coffee, java.

PLANT DESCRIPTION:   A tropical evergreen shrub growing 10 to 15 feet in height mostly in the shade of other trees. The dark, glossy, thin green leaves are 3 to 6 inches long. The star-shaped, lightly

* See Chapter 10 for botanical information.

scented white flowers develop into ¼-inch-long 2-seeded berries called "cherries."

WHERE IT GROWS: In tropical areas of the world, usually at high altitudes.

PART USED: Roasted beans.

87. Coffee (*Pan-American Coffee Bureau*)

**Light brown**

## MORDANT 1

| | |
|---|---|
| Potassium dichromate | 2 tablespoons |
| Water | 2 gallons |

Dissolve the potassium dichromate in the water, and bring to a boil. Add the wet wool, and boil gently for 1 hour. Hang up to dry.

## MORDANT 2

| | |
|---|---|
| Alum | 1 cup |
| Cream of tartar | ¼ cup |
| Water | 2 gallons |

Dissolve the alum and cream of tartar in the water. Bring to a boil, and add the wet wool. Boil gently for 1 hour. Hang up to dry.

**Tan**

## DYE BATH

| | |
|---|---|
| Coffee, ground | 1¾ pounds |
| Water | |

Cover the coffee with water, and boil for 20 minutes. Strain, and discard the coffee grounds. Add cold water to the liquid to make 2 gallons. Bring to a boil, and add the dampened, mordanted wool. Boil gently for 30 minutes. If mordant 2 is used, transfer to a bath containing:

| | |
|---|---|
| Copperas | 1½ teaspoons |
| Water, boiling | 2 gallons |

Boil gently for 10 minutes. Rinse and dry.

## COMMON BARBERRY *Berberis vulgaris* L.

OTHER NAMES: American barberry, dragon grape, guild tree, jaundice barberry, jaundice-tree, pepperidge-bush, sow berry, wood-sour, yellow root.

PLANT DESCRIPTION: A perennial with yellow inner bark and wood, growing from 3 to 8 feet in height. The thick, smooth ½-inch-long leaves are toothed. The yellow flowers grow on short flower stalks. The fruit is an oblong scarlet berry.

WHERE IT GROWS: New England and Northeastern states west to Iowa and Montana. It generally grows in dry open areas.

PART USED: Roots.

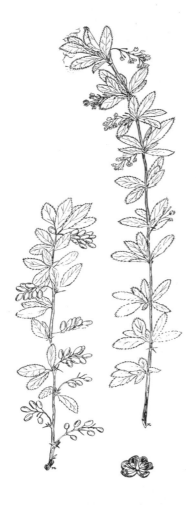

88. Common Barberry
(*U. S. Department of Agriculture*)

**Dark tan**

## MORDANT

| Alum | 1 cup |
| Cream of tartar | ¼ cup |
| Water | 2 gallons |

Dissolve the alum and cream of tartar in the water. Bring to a boil, and add the wet wool. Boil gently for 30 minutes. Hang up to dry.

## DYE BATH

| Barberry roots | 2 gallons |
| Water | |

Chop the roots, cover with water, and soak for 6 hours or overnight.

Then boil for 1 hour and strain. Discard the roots and add cold water to the liquid to make 2 gallons. Bring to a boil and add the dampened, mordanted wool. Boil gently for 30 minutes. Rinse and dry.

## COTTON *Gossypium* spp.

PLANT DESCRIPTION: An annual or perennial shrub growing from 2 to 10 feet in height. It is usually cultivated for the cotton boll or fiber which surrounds the seeds.

WHERE IT GROWS: It is a major crop in the South and Southwest states.

PART USED: Flowers.

89. Cotton (*Department of Crop Science, North Carolina State University*)

**Yellow-tan**

### MORDANT

(For wool)

| | |
|---|---|
| Alum | 1 cup |
| Cream of tartar | ¼ cup |
| Water | 2 gallons |

Dissolve the alum and cream of tartar in the water. Bring to a boil, and add the wet wool. Boil gently for 1 hour. Hang up to dry.

|  |  |
|---|---|
| (For cotton) | |
| Alum | 2 cups |
| Washing soda | ½ cup |
| Water | |
| Tannic acid | 2 tablespoons |

Dissolve 1 cup of the alum and ¼ cup of the washing soda in 2 gallons of water. Add the wet cotton, and bring to a boil. Boil gently for 1 hour. Let the cotton remain in the bath overnight.

The next day bring 2 gallons of water to a boil and add the tannic acid. Remove the cotton from the water that it has been sitting in, squeeze gently, and add to the hot bath containing the tannic acid. Boil gently for 1 hour, stirring frequently. Let the cotton remain in this overnight.

The next day dissolve the remaining cup of alum and ¼ cup of washing soda in 2 gallons of hot water. Remove the cotton from the pot it has been sitting in and rinse. Add the cotton to the bath containing the alum and washing soda, and boil gently for 1 hour, stirring occasionally. Let the cotton remain in the bath overnight.

The next day squeeze the cotton out, and hang up to dry.


**Tan**                              DYE BATH

|  |  |
|---|---|
| Cotton flowers, dry | ½ gallon |
| Water | |

Cover the flowers with water, and boil for 40 minutes. Strain, and discard the flowers. Add cold water to the liquid to make 2 gallons. Bring to a boil, and add the dampened, mordanted wool or cotton. Boil gently for 35 minutes. Transfer to a bath containing:

|  |  |
|---|---|
| Potassium dichromate | 1½ teaspoons |
| Vinegar | ⅓ cup |
| Water, boiling | 2 gallons |

Boil gently for 10 minutes. Rinse and dry.

## CUTCH *Acacia* spp.

OTHER NAMES: Acacia, cassil, catchau, kangaroo-throw, papinac, wattle, una de gatu.

PLANT DESCRIPTION: Trees or shrubs, some with thorns, very small fragrant yellow flowers, compound leaves, typical legume pods from 1 to 6 inches long.

WHERE IT GROWS: Mainly found wild in California, some species occur in Texas, New Mexico, and Arizona into Mexico, generally at higher elevations, above 3,500 feet. It is cultivated in India as a commercial crop.

PART USED: Dried leaves, which are processed and called cutch.

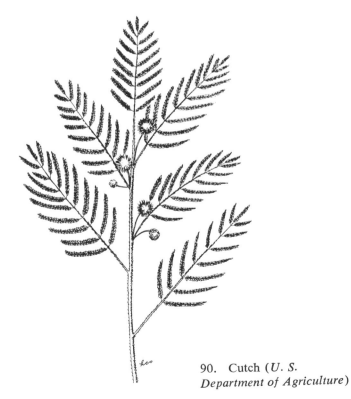

90. Cutch (*U. S. Department of Agriculture*)

**Dark brown**  MORDANT

For wool or cotton, none required.

DYE BATH

| | |
|---|---|
| Cutch | 4 ounces |
| Water | |
| Copper sulfate | 2 tablespoons |
| Potassium dichromate | 2 tablespoons |

Combine the wet, unmordanted goods with 2 gallons of cold water and bring to a boil. Combine the cutch and copper sulfate in 2 gallons of water, and bring to a boil. Transfer the goods from the boiling water to the bath containing the cutch and the copper sulfate. Remove the pot from the heat, and let the goods sit in the bath overnight.

The next day bring 2 gallons of water to a boil, and add the potassium dichromate. Remove the goods from the pot which it has been sitting in and squeeze the excess water from it. Add the goods to the pot containing the potassium dichromate. Boil gently for 30 minutes. Rinse and dry.

## DAHLIA *Dahlia* spp.

PLANT DESCRIPTION:  An erect branching perennial or annual that is a garden favorite that may grow quite tall but usually is from 2 to 4 feet in height. The flowers have yellow centers with pink, red, purple, or white petals.

WHERE IT GROWS:  A native of Guatemala and Mexico, it grows all over the United States.

PARTS USED:  Flowers, roots.

91.  Dahlia (*U. S.*
*Department of Agriculture*)

**Medium brown**                MORDANT

| | |
|---|---|
| Alum | 1 cup |
| Cream of tartar | ¼ cup |
| Water | 2 gallons |

Dissolve the alum and cream of tartar in the water. Bring to a boil, and add the wet wool. Boil gently for 1 hour. Let cool in the water, and then hang up to dry.

DYE BATH

| | |
|---|---|
| Dahlia flowers, roots | 2 gallons (fresh) |
| Water | |

Chop the roots and flowers, and cover with water. Soak overnight. The next day boil for 30 minutes. Strain, and discard the flowers and roots. Add cold water to the liquid to make 2 gallons. Bring to a boil, and add the dampened, mordanted wool. Boil gently for 30 minutes. Rinse and dry.

## EASTERN HEMLOCK *Tsuga canadensis* (L.) Carr.

OTHER NAMES: Canadian hemlock, common hemlock, hemlock fir, hemlock spruce, red hemlock, spruce, spruce pine, tanbark-tree, water spruce, weeping spruce, white hemlock, Wisconsin white hemlock.

PLANT DESCRIPTION: An aromatic evergreen growing to 100 feet in height, with branches that markedly droop. The branches are hairy, yellowish brown and the needles are dark green above and silvery below, ¼ to ¾ inch long.

WHERE IT GROWS: Found in Southeastern Canada, Minnesota, south to Maryland, Georgia, and Alabama. This tree prefers high elevations and moist areas.

PART USED: Bark.

92. Eastern Hemlock
(*U. S. Forest Service*)

**Dark rose-tan**

## MORDANT

(For wool)
| | |
|---|---|
| Alum | 1 cup |
| Cream of tartar | ¼ cup |
| Water | 2 gallons |

Dissolve the alum and cream of tartar in the water. Bring to a boil, and add the wet wool. Boil gently for 1 hour. Hang up to dry. If desired, 2 tablespoons of potassium dichromate can be substituted for the alum and cream of tartar.

**Rose-tan**

(For cotton)
| | |
|---|---|
| Alum | 2 cups |
| Washing soda | ½ cup |
| Tannic acid | 2 tablespoons |
| Water | |

Dissolve 1 cup of the alum and ¼ cup of the washing soda in 2 gallons of water. Add the wet cotton, and bring to a boil. Boil gently for 1 hour. Let the cotton cool in the bath overnight.

The next day bring 2 gallons of water to a boil and add the tannic acid. Remove the cotton from the water that it has been sitting in, squeeze gently, and add to the hot bath containing the tannic acid. Boil gently for 1 hour, stirring frequently. Let the cotton remain in this overnight.

The next day dissolve the remaining cup of alum and ¼ cup of washing soda in 2 gallons of hot water. Remove the cotton from the pot it has been sitting in and rinse. Add the cotton to the bath containing the alum and washing soda, and boil gently for 1 hour, stirring occasionally. Let the cotton remain in the bath overnight.

The next day squeeze the cotton out and hang up to dry.

## DYE BATH

| | |
|---|---|
| Hemlock bark | 2½ gallons |
| Water | |

Chop the bark, cover with water, and soak overnight. The next day boil for 2 hours. Strain, and discard the bark. Add cold water to the liquid to make 2 gallons. Bring to a boil, and add the dampened, mordanted wool or cotton. Boil gently for 30 minutes. Rinse and dry.

## HICKORY *Carya ovata, cordiformis, tomentosa,* and others

OTHER NAMES: Big-bud hickory, bitternut, kingnut, mockernut, pignut, shagbark, shagbark hickory, swamp hickory, white-heart hickory.

PLANT DESCRIPTION: These valuable timber trees, which grow to 120 feet in height, have smooth gray bark when young that becomes rough with age. The leaves are made up of leaflets from 7 to 9 in number, are 3 to 8 inches long, with soft hairs beneath. The fruits are either gray or brown, round to ovoid, from 1½ to 3 inches long.

93. Bitternut Hickory (*U. S. Forest Service*)     93a.  (*U. S. Forest Service*)

WHERE IT GROWS:   Quebec to New York, Massachusetts, west to Minnesota, Nebraska, and Oklahoma, south to Tennessee, Florida, Louisiana, and Texas. It is found in all sorts of habitats.

PARTS USED:   Bark, hulls.

OTHER COLOR:   Yellow.

## MORDANT 1

| Alum | 1 cup |
| Cream of tartar | ¼ cup |
| Water | 2 gallons |

Dissolve the alum and cream of tartar in the water. Bring to a boil, and add the wet wool. Boil gently for 1 hour. Hang up to dry.

## MORDANT 2

(For wool)

| Potassium dichromate | 2 tablespoons |
| Water | 2 gallons |

Dissolve the potassium dichromate in the water, and bring to a boil. Add the wet wool, and boil gently for 1 hour. Hang up to dry.

## MORDANT 3

(For cotton)

| Alum | 2 cups |
| Washing soda | ½ cup |
| Tannic acid | 2 tablespoons |
| Water | |

Dissolve 1 cup of the alum and ¼ cup of the washing soda in 2 gallons of water. Add the wet cotton, and bring to a boil. Boil gently for 1 hour. Let the cotton cool in the bath overnight.

The next day bring 2 gallons of water to a boil and add the tannic acid. Remove the cotton from the water that it has been sitting in, squeeze gently, and add to the hot bath containing the tannic acid. Boil gently for 1 hour, stirring frequently. Let the cotton remain in this overnight.

The next day dissolve the remaining cup of alum and ¼ cup of washing soda in 2 gallons of hot water. Remove the cotton from the water it has been sitting in and rinse. Add the cotton to the bath containing the alum and washing soda, and boil gently for 1 hour, stirring occasionally. Let the cotton remain in the bath overnight.

**Dark yellow-tan**  DYE BATH 1

| Hickory bark | 2 gallons |
|---|---|
| Water | |

Chop the bark, cover with water, and soak overnight. The next day boil for 1 hour. Strain, and discard the bark. Add cold water to the liquid to make 2 gallons. Bring to a boil, and add the dampened, mordanted wool or cotton. Boil gently for 30 minutes. Transfer to a bath containing:

| Potassium dichromate | 1½ teaspoons |
|---|---|
| Vinegar | ⅓ cup |
| Water, boiling | 2 gallons |

Boil gently for 10 minutes. Rinse and dry. (If desired, the mordant and afterbath can be eliminated and ¼ cup of alum added to the dye bath just before the wool is added.)

**Light brown**  DYE BATH 2

| Hickory nut shells, green | 2 gallons |
|---|---|
| Water | |

Cover the hulls with water, and soak overnight. The next day boil for 45 minutes. Strain, and discard the hulls. Add cold water to the liquid to make 2 gallons. Bring to a boil, and add the dampened, mordanted wool or cotton. Boil gently for 30 minutes. Transfer to a bath containing:

| Potassium dichromate | 1½ teaspoons |
|---|---|
| Vinegar | ⅓ cup |
| Water, boiling | 2 gallons |

Boil gently for 10 minutes. Rinse and dry.

## INDIAN HEMP *Apocynum cannabinum* L.*

**Dark tan**

### MORDANT

Alum     1 cup
Water    2 gallons

Dissolve the alum in the water, and bring to a boil. Add the wet wool, and boil gently for 1 hour. Hang up to dry.

### DYE BATH

Indian hemp plant     2 quarts
Water

Chop the plants, cover with water, and soak overnight. The next day boil for 30 minutes. Strain, and discard the plants. Add cold water to the liquid to make 2 gallons. Bring to a boil, and add the dampened, mordanted wool. Boil gently for 45 minutes. Rinse and dry.

## MADRONA *Arbutus menziesii* Pursh.

OTHER NAME:  Madrone.

PLANT DESCRIPTION:  This evergreen tree grows to over 100 feet in height. Leaves are 2 to 6 inches long, roundish to oblong, dark shiny green above, fuzzy beneath. The white flowers, ¼ inch long, grow on long-stemmed clusters. The fruit is a dark orange berry.

WHERE IT GROWS:  It is a Western tree found from California to Oregon and Washington.

PART USED:  Bark.

* See Chapter 13 for botanical information.

94. Madrona
(*U. S. Forest Service*)

94a.  (*U. S. Forest Service*)

## MORDANT

None required.

**Brown**                          DYE BATH

          Madrona bark     2 gallons
          Water

Chop the bark, cover with water, and soak overnight. The next day boil for 1 hour and strain. Discard the bark, and add cold water to the liquid to make 2 gallons. Bring to a boil, and add the wet, un-mordanted wool. Boil gently for 40 minutes. Rinse and dry.

## MAPLE *Acer* spp.*

**Rose-tan**

### MORDANT

| | |
|---|---|
| Alum | 1 cup |
| Cream of tartar | ¼ cup |
| Water | 2 gallons |

Dissolve the alum and cream of tartar in the water. Bring to a boil, and add the wet wool. Boil gently for 1 hour. Hang up to dry. If desired, 2 tablespoons of potassium dichromate can be substituted for the alum and cream of tartar.

### DYE BATH

| | |
|---|---|
| Maple bark | 2½ gallons |
| Water | |

Chop the bark, cover with water, and soak overnight. The next day boil for 2 hours. Strain, and discard the bark. Add cold water to the liquid to make 2 gallons. Bring to a boil, and add the dampened, mordanted wool. Boil gently for 30 minutes. If the alum mordant was used, transfer to a bath containing:

| | |
|---|---|
| Copper sulfate | 1½ teaspoons |
| Water, boiling | 2 gallons |

Boil gently for 10 minutes. Rinse and dry.

## MARIGOLD *Tagetes* spp.

PLANT DESCRIPTION:  A wide number of very popular annuals growing from 1 to 2 feet in height, with leaves which are rather unpleasant or strong smelling. The long-lasting flowers are usually yellow or orange.

* See Chapter 14 for botanical information.

95.  Marigold (*U. S. Department of Agriculture*)

WHERE IT GROWS:    They are cultivated all over the United States as a garden flower.

PART USED:    Leaves.

**Yellow-tan**                       MORDANT

                  (For wool)

| | |
|---|---|
| Alum | 1 cup |
| Cream of tartar | 2 tablespoons |
| Water | 2 gallons |

Dissolve the alum and cream of tartar in the water. Bring to a boil, and add the wet wool. Boil gently for 1 hour. Hang up to dry.

**Dark tan**

                  (For cotton)

| | |
|---|---|
| Alum | 2 cups |
| Washing soda | ½ cup |
| Tannic acid | 2 tablespoons |
| Water | |

Dissolve 1 cup of the alum and ¼ cup of the washing soda in 2 gallons of water. Add the wet cotton, and bring to a boil. Boil gently for 1 hour. Let the cotton remain in the bath overnight.

The next day bring 2 gallons of water to a boil and add the tannic acid. Remove the cotton from the water that it has been sitting in; squeeze gently and add to the hot bath containing the tannic acid. Boil gently for 1 hour, stirring frequently. Let the cotton remain in the bath overnight.

The next day dissolve the remaining cup of alum and ¼ cup of washing soda in 2 gallons of hot water. Remove the cotton from the pot that it has been sitting in and rinse. Add the cotton to the bath containing the alum and washing soda, and boil gently for 1 hour, stirring occasionally. Let the cotton remain in the bath overnight.

The next day squeeze the cotton out and hang up to dry.

### DYE BATH

| | |
|---|---|
| Marigold flowers, fresh | 2 gallons |
| or dried | 1½ gallons |
| Water | |

Cover the flowers with water, and boil for 1 hour. Strain, and discard the flowers. Add cold water to the liquid to make 2 gallons. Bring to a boil, and add the dampened, mordanted wool or cotton. Boil gently for 25 minutes. Transfer to a bath containing:

| | |
|---|---|
| Potassium dichromate | 1½ teaspoons |
| Vinegar | ⅓ cup |
| Water, boiling | 2 gallons |

Boil gently for 10 minutes. Rinse and dry.

## MOUNTAIN LAUREL *Kalmia latifolia* L.

OTHER NAMES:    Calico bush, ivy bush, spoonwood.

PLANT DESCRIPTION:    A densely growing bush or small tree sometimes growing to 20 feet or more in height. The evergreen leaves are usually alternate, narrowed at both ends, 2 to 5 inches long, darker green above than below. The flowers, ¾ inch across, are white to rose, with violet markings, and grow on terminal clusters.

96. Mountain Laurel (*Dr. J. Hardin, Botany Department, North Carolina State University*)

WHERE IT GROWS: The species is found east of the Mississippi River in swamps, sandy woods, and clearings.

PART USED: Fresh leaves.

**Yellow-tan**

## MORDANT

| | |
|---|---|
| Potassium dichromate | 2 tablespoons |
| Water | 2 gallons |

Dissolve the potassium dichromate in the water and bring to a boil. Add the wet wool, and boil for 1 hour. Hang up to dry.

## DYE BATH

| | |
|---|---|
| Mountain laurel leaves, fresh | 3 gallons |
| Water | |

Chop the leaves, cover with water, and soak overnight. The next day boil for 20 minutes. Strain, and discard the leaves. Add cold water to the liquid to make 2 gallons. Bring to a boil, and add the dampened, mordanted wool. Boil gently for 30 minutes. Rinse and dry.

## MOUNTAIN MINT *Pycnanthemum tenuifolium* Schrader

OTHER NAME:   Basil.

PLANT DESCRIPTION:   An upright, smooth plant with quadrangular stems, and foliage with a pungent, mintlike smell, growing to 3 feet in height. The long, narrow leaves are ⅛ to ¼ inch wide, and taper to a point. The tiny white or purplish flowers grow in dense whorls which form terminal heads.

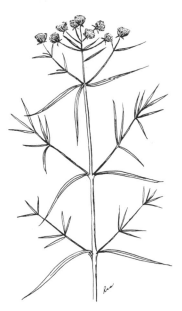

97.   Mountain Mint (*U. S. Department of Agriculture*)

WHERE IT GROWS:   This plant and close relatives are found growing from New England to Florida, and west to Texas, Colorado, and New Mexico. It does well in damp areas, bogs, pine barrens, and pastures.

PARTS USED:   Stalks, leaves, flowers, dried or fresh.

OTHER COLOR:   Yellow.

**Light tan**

## MORDANT

| | |
|---|---|
| Potassium dichromate | 2 tablespoons |
| Water | 2 gallons |

Dissolve the potassium dichromate in the water, and bring to a boil. Add the wet wool, and boil gently for 1 hour. Hang up to dry.

## DYE BATH

| | |
|---|---|
| Mountain mint, stalks, flowers, leaves | 1½ gallons |
| Water | |

Chop the plants, and boil for 30 minutes. Strain, and discard the plants. Add cold water to the liquid to make 2 gallons. Bring to a boil, and add the dampened, mordanted wool. Boil gently for 30 minutes. Rinse and dry.

## NEW JERSEY TEA *Ceanothus americanus* L.

OTHER NAMES: Jersey tea ceanothus, New Jersey tea tree, redroot, wild snowball.

¼"

98. New Jersey Tea (*U. S. Forest Service*)

1"

PLANT DESCRIPTION:   A shrub growing to 3½ feet in height. The toothed leaves are green, smooth above, and gray and hairy below, to 4 inches in length. The white flowers occur in clusters 1 to 2 inches long. During the Revolution the leaves were used as a replacement for tea.

WHERE IT GROWS:   New England to Minnesota, south to Florida, Alabama, and Texas. It grows in dry areas, open woods, rocky slopes, hardwood and pine forests, and in dry fields.

PART USED:   Roots.

**Dark tan**                              MORDANT

None required.

## DYE BATH

New Jersey tea roots     1 gallon
Water

Chop the roots, cover with water, and soak overnight. The next day boil for 45 minutes. Strain, and discard the roots. Add cold water to the liquid to make 2 gallons. Bring to a boil, and add the wet, unmordanted wool. Boil gently for 50 minutes. Rinse and dry.

## OAK *Quercus* spp.*

## MORDANT

Alum                  1 cup
Cream of tartar       ¼ cup
Water                 2 gallons

Dissolve the alum and cream of tartar in the water. Bring to a boil, and add the wet wool. Boil gently for 1 hour. Hang up to dry.

* See Chapter 10 for botanical information.

**Tan**
## DYE BATH 1

    Oak bark (any species)   2 gallons
    Water

    Chop the bark, cover with water, and soak overnight. The next day boil for 2 hours, and strain. Discard the bark, and add cold water to the liquid to make 2 gallons. Bring to a boil, and add the dampened, mordanted wool. Boil gently for 30 minutes. Transfer to a bath containing:

        Potassium dichromate    1½ teaspoons
        Vinegar              ⅓ cup
        Water               2 gallons

    Boil gently for 10 minutes. Rinse and dry.

**Light brown**
## DYE BATH 2

    Quercitron extract    2 tablespoons
    Water             2 gallons

    Dissolve the extract in the water, and bring to a boil. Add the dampened, mordanted wool. Boil gently for 30 minutes. Transfer to a bath containing:

        Potassium dichromate    1½ teaspoons
        Vinegar              ⅓ cup
        Water, boiling      2 gallons

    Boil gently for 10 minutes. Rinse and dry.

**Gray-tan**
## DYE BATH 3

    Acorns    1½ gallons
    Alum     ½ cup
    Water

    Crush the acorns, cover with water, and boil for 2 hours. Strain, and discard the acorns. Add cold water to the liquid to make 2 gallons. Bring to a boil, and add the alum. Stir well, and add the dampened, mordanted wool. Boil gently for 30 minutes. Rinse and dry.

## OSAGE ORANGE *Maclura pomifera* Schneid.*

**Medium brown**                MORDANT

(For wool)
Alum                1 cup
Cream of tartar     ¼ cup
Water               2 gallons

Dissolve the alum and cream of tartar in the water. Bring to a boil, and add the wet wool. Boil gently for 1 hour. Hang up to dry.

**Yellow-tan**

(For cotton)
Alum                2 cups
Washing soda        ½ cup
Tannic acid         2 tablespoons
Water

Dissolve 1 cup of the alum and ¼ cup of the washing soda in 2 gallons of water. Add the wet cotton, and bring to a boil. Boil gently for 1 hour. Let the cotton stay in the bath overnight.

The next day bring 2 gallons of water to a boil, and add the tannic acid. Remove the cotton from the water that it has been sitting in, squeeze gently, and add to the hot bath containing the tannic acid. Boil gently for 1 hour, stirring frequently. Let the cotton remain in this overnight.

The next day dissolve the remaining cup of alum and ¼ cup of washing soda in 2 gallons of hot water. Remove the cotton from the pot it has been sitting in and rinse. Add the cotton to the bath containing the alum and washing soda, and boil gently for 1 hour, stirring occasionally. Let the cotton remain in the bath overnight.

The next day squeeze the cotton out and hang up to dry.

### DYE BATH

Osage orange extract     2 tablespoons
Water                    2 gallons

Dissolve the extract in the water. Bring to a boil, and add the

* See Chapter 7 for botanical information.

dampened, mordanted wool or cotton. Boil gently for 30 minutes. Transfer to a bath containing:

| | |
|---|---|
| Potassium dichromate | 1½ teaspoons |
| Vinegar | ⅓ cup |
| Water, boiling | 2 gallons |

Boil gently for 10 minutes. Rinse and dry.

## PEAR *Pyrus communis* L.

OTHER NAME:   Common pear.

PLANT DESCRIPTION:   Another familiar friend grown in orchards, back yards, and often found near abandoned farms as a testimony to the love of the land of some forgotton settler long since gone. In the Daniel Boone National Forest in Kentucky we often harvested large, hard, perfumed fruits from the orchards of a long-gone farmer.

WHERE IT GROWS:   Man carried it with him in his colonizing of temperate areas, and at high elevations in warmer areas.

PART USED:   Leaves.

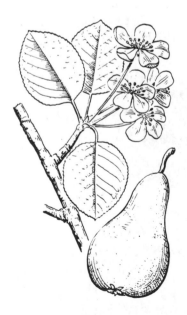

99.   Pear (*University of West Virginia, from* FLORA OF WEST VIRGINIA)

**Yellow-tan**

## MORDANT

| | |
|---|---|
| Alum | 1 cup |
| Cream of tartar | ¼ cup |
| Water | 2 gallons |

Dissolve the alum and cream of tartar in the water. Bring to a boil, and add the wet wool. Boil gently for 30 minutes. Hang up to dry.

## DYE BATH

| | |
|---|---|
| Pear leaves | 2 gallons |
| Water | |

Chop the leaves, cover with water, and soak overnight. The next day boil for 1 hour. Strain, and discard the leaves. Add cold water to the liquid to make 2 gallons. Bring to a boil, and add the dampened, mordanted wool. Boil gently for 30 minutes. Rinse and dry.

## PECAN *Carya illinoensis* Koch.

PLANT DESCRIPTION:    A tree growing to 170 feet in height, with deeply furrowed, ridged bark that becomes rough or scaly on older trees. The lance-shaped leaves are smooth above and hairy beneath, from 3 to 7 inches long with toothed edges, and grow in groups of 11 to 17 per branch. The nut, which grows in groups of 3 to 10, is round

100.    Pecan (*U. S. Forest Service*)

to oblong, thin-shelled, either gray or brown, with black markings, 2 to 3 inches long.

WHERE IT GROWS: It grows in a wide range of sites, and as a cultivated crop. It grows from Indiana to Iowa, south to Alabama, Mississippi, Louisiana, Texas, and Mexico.

PARTS USED: Hulls, blossoms.

## **Brown** MORDANT

*METHOD 1*

| | |
|---|---|
| Alum | ½ cup |
| Cream of tartar | ½ cup |
| Water | 2 gallons |

Dissolve the alum and cream of tartar in the water. Bring to a boil, and add the wet wool. Boil gently for 1 hour. Hang up to dry.

## DYE BATH

| | |
|---|---|
| Pecan blossoms, fresh or dried | 1½ gallons |
| Water | |

Cover the blossoms with water, and boil for 30 minutes. Strain, and discard the blossoms. Add cold water to the liquid to make 2 gallons. Bring to a boil, and add the dampened, mordanted wool. Boil gently for 25 minutes. Rinse and dry.

## **Dark tan** MORDANT

*METHOD 2*

For wool none required.

| (For cotton) | |
|---|---|
| Alum | 1 cup |
| Washing soda | ¼ cup |
| Water | 2 gallons |

Dissolve the alum and washing soda in the water. Bring to a boil, and add the wet cotton. Boil gently for 45 minutes. Hang up to dry.

## DYE BATH

| | |
|---|---|
| Pecan hulls | 1½ gallons |
| Alum | ½ cup |
| Water | |

Cover the hulls with water and boil for 2 hours. Strain, and discard the hulls. Add cold water to the liquid to make 2 gallons. Bring to a boil, and add the alum. Stir well, and add the wet, unmordanted wool or the dampened, mordanted cotton. Boil gently for 50 minutes. For cotton only, transfer to a bath containing:

| | |
|---|---|
| Copperas | 2 teaspoons |
| Water, boiling | 2 gallons |

Boil gently for 10 minutes. Rinse and dry.

## PRIVET *Ligustrum vulgare* L.

OTHER NAMES:   Common privet, prim.

PLANT DESCRIPTION:   A small tree or shrub growing to 15 feet in height, usually planted as an ornamental hedge. The lance-shaped leaves are 1 to 2½ inches long. The tiny white flowers grow in pyramidal shaped clusters at the ends of the branches. The fruit is a small black berry. There are a number of introduced ornamental species grown in gardens.

WHERE IT GROWS:   This species grows in Canada, New England, south to Ohio and Michigan, and North Carolina. Cultivated species are found all over Canada and the United States, wild or escaped plants occur in open, dry wooded areas, roadsides, and thickets.

PARTS USED:   Leaves and clippings.

OTHER COLOR:   Yellow.

**Tan**

## MORDANT

| | |
|---|---|
| Alum | ¾ cup |
| Cream of tartar | ¼ cup |
| Water | 2 gallons |

Dissolve the alum and cream of tartar in the water. Bring to a boil, and add the wet wool. Boil gently for 1 hour. Hang up to dry.

## DYE BATH

| | |
|---|---|
| Privet clippings | 2 gallons |
| Water | |

Cover the clippings with water and soak overnight. The next day boil for 1 hour. Strain, and discard the clippings. Add cold water to the liquid to make 2 gallons. Bring to a boil, and add the dampened, mordanted wool. Boil gently for 45 minutes. Rinse and dry.

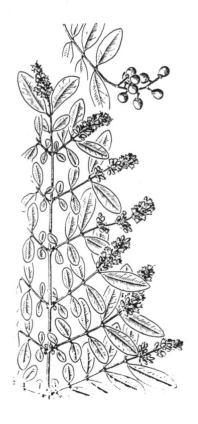

101. Privet (*University of West Virginia, from* FLORA OF WEST VIRGINIA)

## SUMAC *Rhus glabra* L.,* *Rhus copallina* L.

**Yellow-tan**                    MORDANT

(For cotton)
Alum            1 cup
Washing soda    ¼ cup
Water           2 gallons

Dissolve the alum and washing soda in the water. Bring to a boil, and add the wet cotton. Boil gently for 1 hour. Hang up to dry.

(For wool)
In the above recipe substitute cream of tartar for the washing soda, and reduce the alum by half.

### DYE BATH

Sumac berries, ripe    1 gallon
Water

Crush the berries, cover with water, and soak overnight. The next day boil for 1 hour. Strain, and discard the berries. Add cold water to the liquid to make 2 gallons. Bring to a boil, and add the dampened, mordanted wool or cotton. Boil gently for 30 minutes. Rinse and dry.

## SOURWOOD *Nyssa sylvatica* Marsh.**

**Yellow-tan**                    MORDANT

Alum             1 cup
Cream of tartar  ¼ cup
Water            2 gallons

Dissolve the alum and cream of tartar in the water. Bring to a boil, and add the wet wool. Boil gently for 1 hour. Hang up to dry.

* See Chapter 13 for botanical information.
** See Chapter 13 for botanical information.

## DYE BATH

Sourwood bark    2½ gallons
Water

Chop the bark, cover with water, and soak overnight. The next day boil for 2 hours, and strain. Discard the bark, and add cold water to the liquid to make 2 gallons. Bring to a boil and add the dampened, mordanted wool. Boil gently for 30 minutes. Rinse and dry.

## SUNFLOWER *Helianthus* spp.

PLANT DESCRIPTION:  A friendly and familiar group of plants growing to 15 feet in height, with a stout, rough stem branching at the top, the pointed leaves, rough on both sides. The yellow flowers are 3 to 6 inches across, and have black petals.

102. Sunflower (*Colorado State University, from* WEEDS OF COLORADO)

WHERE IT GROWS:   It is found in all the states, Canada, and Mexico. It is often cultivated as a garden ornamental, as an oil crop, and for its nourishing seed. It prefers open sunny areas.

PART USED:   Flowers.

OTHER COLOR:   Yellow.

**Tan**

### MORDANT

| | |
|---|---|
| Alum | 1 cup |
| Cream of tartar | ¼ cup |
| Water | 2 gallons |

Dissolve the alum and cream of tartar in the water. Bring to a boil, and add the wet wool. Boil gently for 1 hour. Let the wool stay in the water overnight. The next day hang up to dry.

### DYE BATH

| | |
|---|---|
| Sunflowers, fresh or dried | 1 gallon |
| Water | |

Cover the flowers with water, and boil for 40 minutes. Strain, and discard the flowers. Add cold water to the liquid to make 2 gallons. Bring to a boil, and add the dampened, mordanted wool. Boil gently for 30 minutes. Transfer to a bath containing:

| | |
|---|---|
| Potassium dichromate | 1½ teaspoons |
| Vinegar | ⅓ cup |
| Water, boiling | 2 gallons |

Boil gently for 10 minutes. Rinse and dry.

## TEA *Thea sinensis* L.

PLANT DESCRIPTION:   A shrub or tree grown in tropical or sub-tropical parts of the world. The smooth leaves are 2 to 5 inches long and are plucked for tea.

WHERE IT GROWS:   China, India, and in other parts of the world. At Charles Towne Landing, Charleston, South Carolina, a fascinating garden of early colonial crops includes tea plants grown experimentally during colonial times.

PART USED:   Leaves from so-called black tea.

103.   Tea (*Tea Council of the U.S.A.*)

**Rose-tan**                    MORDANT

*METHOD 1*

None required.

DYE BATH

Black tea        2 cups
Water

Cover the tea with water, and soak overnight. The next day boil for 15 minutes, and strain. Discard the tea, and add cold water to the liquid to make 2 gallons. Bring to a boil, and add the wet, unmordanted wool. Boil gently for 30 minutes. Rinse and dry.

## MORDANT

*METHOD 2*

| | |
|---|---|
| Alum | 1 cup |
| Cream of tartar | ¼ cup |
| Water | 2 gallons |

Dissolve the alum and cream of tartar in the water. Bring to a boil, and add the wet wool. Boil gently for 1 hour. Hang up to dry. If desired, 2 tablespoons of potassium dichromate can be substituted for the alum and cream of tartar.

## DYE BATH

| | |
|---|---|
| Black tea | 1¾ cups |
| Water | |

Cover the tea with water, and boil for 15 minutes. Strain, and discard the tea. Add cold water to the liquid to make 2 gallons. Bring to a boil, and add the dampened, mordanted wool. Boil gently for 30 minutes. If the alum and cream of tartar mordant was used, transfer to a bath containing:

| | |
|---|---|
| Copperas | 1½ teaspoons |
| Water, boiling | 2 gallons |

Boil gently for 10 minutes. Rinse and dry.

## TOBACCO *Nicotiana* spp.

PLANT DESCRIPTION:    An annual reaching 5 feet in height, with large leaves to 12 inches long with fuzz. Flowers appear at the growing apex of the plant.

WHERE IT GROWS:    It is found domesticated in most parts of the United States, from Connecticut to garden plants in New Mexico and Arizona, as well as large farms in Kentucky, Virginia, and the

Carolinas. It grows best as a crop in the open field with sun and adequate rainfall.

PART USED:   Leaves, dried.

104.  Tobacco
(*Department of
Crop Science,
North Carolina
State University*)

**Tan**

## MORDANT

None required.

## DYE BATH

| | |
|---|---|
| Tobacco, cured | 1 pound |
| Alum | ½ cup |
| Cream of tartar | ¼ cup |
| Water | |

Chop the tobacco, cover with water, and soak overnight. The next day boil for 1½ hours. Strain, and discard the tobacco. Add cold water to the liquid to make 2 gallons. Bring to a boil, and stir in the alum and cream of tartar. Add the wet, unmordanted wool. Boil gently for 45 minutes. Rinse and dry.

## WHITE SASSAFRAS *Sassafras albidum* (Nutal) Nees.

OTHER NAMES: Ague tree, cinnamon wood, common sassafras, red sassafras, saxigras, smelling stick.

PLANT DESCRIPTION: A familiar forest tree growing to 125 feet in height. The aromatic leaves, 3 to 5 inches long, are ovate to elliptical, some are 2- to 3-lobed, while others are entire. The dark blue fruit is ½ inch thick.

105.  Sassafras (*U. S. Forest Service*)      105a.  (*U. S. Forest Service*)

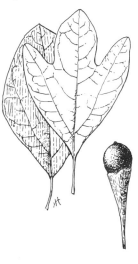

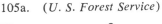

WHERE IT GROWS:   It ranges from New England west to Michigan, south to Florida and Texas, and is usually found in drier areas such as hardwood forests, roadsides, and old fields.

PARTS USED:   Root bark, leaves, twigs, roots.

OTHER COLOR:   Gray.

## **Brown**                    MORDANT

For cotton none required.

| (For wool) | |
|---|---|
| Alum | 1 cup |
| Cream of tartar | ¼ cup |
| Water | 2 gallons |

Dissolve the alum and cream of tartar in the water. Bring to a boil, and add the wet wool. Boil gently for 1 hour. Hang up to dry.

## DYE BATH

| Sassafras root bark, twigs, leaves, roots | 2 gallons |
|---|---|
| Water | |

Chop the plant material, cover with water, and soak overnight. The next day boil for 1 hour. Strain, and discard the plant material. Add cold water to the liquid to make 2 gallons. Bring to a boil, and add the wet, unmordanted cotton or the dampened, mordanted wool. Boil gently for 30 minutes. Rinse and dry. (If desired, the mordant for wool can be eliminated.)

## WILD PLUM *Prunus americana* Marsh.

PLANT DESCRIPTION:   A shrub or tree growing from 25 to 30 feet in height with rough bark. Leaves are toothed, smooth above, fuzzy below and 3 to 4 inches long. The white flowers grow in umbrella-shaped clusters and give rise to orange-red fruit with a hard, flat stone. Many related species, domesticated and introduced, are to be found.

WHERE IT GROWS: The relatives and the wild plum itself can be found wild and cultivated in Southern Canada and all parts of the United States in a variety of habitats.

PART USED: Bark.

106. Wild Plum (*University of West Virginia, from* FLORA OF WEST VIRGINIA)

**Reddish brown**

## MORDANT

| | |
|---|---|
| Alum | 1 cup |
| Cream of tartar | ¼ cup |
| Water | 2 gallons |

Dissolve the alum and cream of tartar in the water. Bring to a boil and add the wet wool. Boil gently for 1 hour. Hang up to dry.

## DYE BATH

| | |
|---|---|
| Plum bark | 2 gallons |
| Water | |

Chop the bark, cover with water, and soak overnight. The next day boil for 1 hour, and strain. Discard the bark, and add cold water to the liquid to make 2 gallons. Bring to a boil, and add the dampened, mordanted wool. Boil gently for 30 minutes. Rinse and dry.

## WILLOW *Salix* spp.

OTHER NAMES: Black willow, Caroline willow, pussy willow, swamp willow, weeping willow, white willow.

PLANT DESCRIPTION: Shrubs as well as trees as tall as 90 feet in height. Leaves of the more familiar species are lance-shaped and most often are alternate. Flowers are catkins—the familiar pussy willows found in early spring in woods. The catkins often are seen opening before or at the same time leaves appear. The varieties hybridize rather readily, bringing new plants into being. There are many imported species used as decoratives.

WHERE IT GROWS: Some members are found from Alaska throughout Canada and all of the states. They seem to be found mostly in damp areas, stream banks, meadows, rich lowlands, borders of woods, and many other habitats.

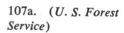

107. Willow (*U. S. Forest Service*)

107a. (*U. S. Forest Service*)

**Rose tan**

## MORDANT

| | |
|---|---|
| Alum | 1 cup |
| Cream of tartar | ¼ cup |
| Water | 2 gallons |

Dissolve the alum and cream of tartar in the water. Bring to a boil, and add the wet wool. Boil gently for 30 minutes. Hang up to dry.

## DYE BATH

| | |
|---|---|
| Willow bark | 2½ gallons |
| Water | |

Chop the bark, cover with water, and soak overnight. The next day boil for 1½ hours. Strain, and discard the bark. Add cold water to the liquid to make 2 gallons. Bring to a boil, and add the dampened, mordanted wool. Boil gently for 30 minutes. Rinse and dry.

# CHAPTER 13

# Black dyes

## ALDER *Alnus* spp.

OTHER NAMES:  Green ash, mountain ash.

PLANT DESCRIPTION:  A shrub or tree growing to 20 feet in height. The round, smooth leaves, 1 to 3 inches long, have finely toothed margins. The greenish-yellow flowers grow in bunches of threes on long stems. The small nuts are about 1 inch long.

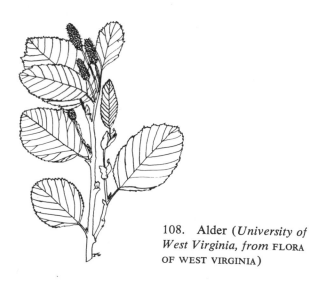

108.  Alder (*University of West Virginia, from* FLORA OF WEST VIRGINIA)

WHERE IT GROWS:   From Alaska through all of Canada, as far south as North Carolina, and in Michigan, Wisconsin, Minnesota. It is often found along streams in mountainous areas and cool woods.

PARTS USED:   Leaves, bark, roots.

OTHER COLORS:   Yellow, green, brown.

## MORDANT

*METHOD 1*

| | |
|---|---|
| Alum | 1 cup |
| Cream of tartar | ¼ cup |
| Water | 2 gallons |

Dissolve the alum and cream of tartar in the water. Bring to a boil, and add the wet wool. Boil gently for 1 hour. Let the wool cool in the water overnight. The next day hang up to dry.

## DYE BATH

| | |
|---|---|
| Alder bark | 1½ quarts |
| Copperas | ¼ cup |
| Water | |

Chop the bark, cover with water, and soak overnight. The next day boil for 1½ hours. Strain and discard the bark. Add cold water to the liquid to make 2 gallons. Bring to a boil, and add the copperas. Stir well, and add the dampened, mordanted wool. Boil gently for 1 hour. Rinse and dry.

## MORDANT

*METHOD 2*

None required.

## DYE BATH

| | |
|---|---|
| Alder bark | 2 quarts |
| Copper sulfate | 2 tablespoons |
| Water | |

Chop the bark, cover with water, and soak overnight. The next day boil for 2 hours. Strain, and discard the bark. Add cold water to the liquid to make 2 gallons. Bring to a boil, and add the copper sulfate. Stir well, and add the wet, unmordanted wool. Boil gently for 1½ hours. Rinse and dry.

## BLACK WALNUT *Juglans nigra* L.

OTHER NAMES:    American walnut, Eastern black walnut.

PLANT DESCRIPTION:    A valuable timber tree growing to more than 130 feet in height with dark brown or black bark, with deep, narrow furrows. The leaflets are pointed, smooth above, and downy below, finely toothed, 2 to 5 inches long, and grow in bunches of 11 to 23 per branch. The smooth, round edible fruits are about 2 inches across, occur in clusters of 2 or 3, and have thick, aromatic shells.

109.   Black Walnut
(*U. S. Forest Service*)

109a.   (*U. S. Forest Service*)

Other walnuts such as the Persian and English walnuts may be substituted for the one we have described.

WHERE IT GROWS:    The tree and its close relatives are found from New England and Southeastern Canada to Florida, Texas, and Arkansas and west to North Dakota and Minnesota. Rich woods and limestone soils are favored sites.

PARTS USED:    Bark, hulls, twigs, leaves.

OTHER COLOR:    Brown.

## MORDANT

None required.

## DYE BATH

Black walnut leaves      2 gallons
Water

Layer the leaves and the wool in a pot. Pour in water to cover, and seal the pot. Let set for 10 days. Remove the wool, and rinse and dry.

## BRAMBLE *Rubus* spp.

OTHER NAMES:    Blackberry, dewberry, raspberry.

PLANT DESCRIPTION:    Most of these are erect, but in some species the stem is prostrate on the ground. The leaves are made up of 3 to 5 leaflets. Some species have stickers on the stems, and others do not.

110.  Bramble
(*U. S. Department of Agriculture*)

The flowers grow on 2-year or older wood, and vary from white to pink. The ripe fruit may be purple, black, or blue.

WHERE IT GROWS:    Members may be found throughout the entire area of Canada and the United States in diverse locations such as thickets, borders of woods, old homesites, wood openings, hillsides, and gravelly slopes.

PARTS USED:    Ripe berries, young shoots.

OTHER COLOR:    Gray.

## MORDANT

| Iron | 3 tablespoons |
|------|---------------|
| Water | 2 gallons |

Dissolve the iron in the water, and add the wet wool. Bring to a boil and boil gently for 1½ hours. Hang up to dry.

## DYE BATH

Green bramble shoots      1¾ gallons
Water

Chop the green shoots, cover with water, and boil for 45 minutes. Strain, and discard the shoots. Add cold water to the liquid to make 2 gallons. Bring to a boil, and add the dampened, mordanted wool. Boil gently for 40 minutes. Rinse and dry.

## BUGLEWEED *Lycopus virginicus* L.

OTHER NAMES:    Buglewort, ditch-horehound, Paul's betony, Virginia horehound, water horehound.

PLANT DESCRIPTION:    A plant that has four-angled, slender, hairy stems and spreads through long leafy runners. The dark green, coarsely toothed leaves are pointed at both ends. The purple to white flowers occur in clusters in leaf axils and with some imagination seems to resemble a bugle.

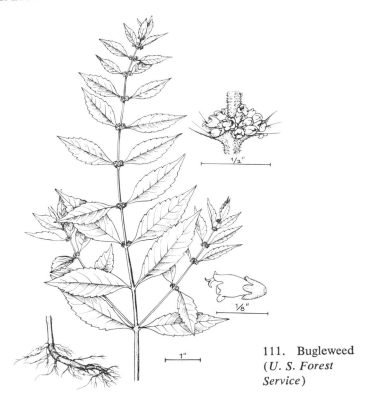

111.  Bugleweed
(*U. S. Forest
Service*)

WHERE IT GROWS:    It is found from New England west to Wisconsin and Minnesota and south to Florida, Georgia, Alabama, and Texas. It is found in wet areas, often clogging ditches.

PARTS USED:   Whole herb.

## MORDANT

| | |
|---|---|
| Alum | ¾ cup |
| Cream of tartar | ¼ cup |
| Water | 2 gallons |

Dissolve the alum and cream of tartar in the water. Bring to a boil, and add the wet wool. Boil gently for 1 hour. Hang up to dry.

## DYE BATH

Bugleweed, fresh    3 gallons
Water

Chop the plants, cover with water, and boil for 30 minutes. Strain, and discard the plants. Add cold water to the liquid to make 2 gallons. Bring to a boil, and add the dampened, mordanted wool. Boil gently for 45 minutes. Rinse and dry.

## INDIAN HEMP *Apocynum cannabinum* L.

OTHER NAMES:   American hemp, amy root, bowman's root, choctaw root, dropsy root, Indian physic, rheumatism weed.

PLANT DESCRIPTION:   A perennial with a tall, smooth stem growing 1 to 5 feet in height. The pale green oblong leaves grow 2 to 4 inches long, pointed at both ends, smooth above and sometimes hairy below. The flowers form clusters at the top of the stem. A seed pod resembling milkweed is formed.

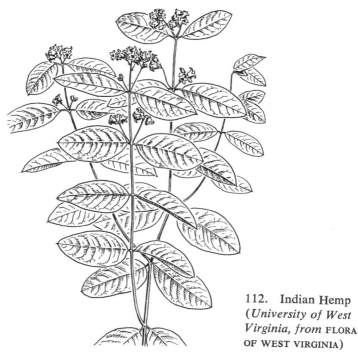

112.  Indian Hemp
(*University of West
Virginia, from* FLORA
OF WEST VIRGINIA)

WHERE IT GROWS:  It is found in Canada and all parts of the United States in a wide range of habitats.

PARTS USED:  Whole plant.

OTHER COLOR:  Brown.

## MORDANT

| Copperas | 3 tablespoons |
| Water | 2 gallons |

Dissolve the copperas in the water, and bring to a boil. Add the wet wool, and boil gently for 1 hour. Hang up to dry.

## DYE BATH

| Indian hemp | 2 quarts |
| Water | |

Chop the plants, cover with water, and soak overnight. The next day boil for 30 minutes. Strain, and discard the plants. Add cold water to the liquid to make 2 gallons. Bring to a boil, and add the dampened, mordanted wool. Boil gently for 50 minutes. Rinse and dry.

## SUMAC *Rhus glabra* L., *Rhus Copallina* L.

OTHER NAMES:  Smooth sumac, common sumac, Pennsylvania sumac, scarlet sumac, shernoke, shoemake, upland sumac, shining sumac.

PLANT DESCRIPTION:  A small tree or shrub with milky sap that grows to 20 feet in height. The leaves range from 1 to 3 feet long, with 10 to 20 toothed leaflets. The greenish flowers grow on flower stalks in dense bunches 4 to 10 inches long and produce pyramidal clusters of red fruits, which are sticky and hairy.

WHERE IT GROWS:  It grows in all states, Canada, Alaska, and Mexico. The plants prefer dry soil, waste areas, edges of woods, pastures, meadows, old fields, power lines, and right of ways.

113. Shining Sumac (*U. S. Forest Service*)

PARTS USED: Berries, stems, twigs, leaves, bark.

OTHER COLORS: Brown, yellow, gray.

## MORDANT

Iron      ¼ cup
Water     2 gallons

Dissolve the iron in the water. Bring to a boil, and rinse the wet wool out in the liquid. Hang up until the wool oxidizes. Then it is ready to be added to the dye bath.

## DYE BATH

Sumac foliage and berries     1 gallon
Water

Crush the plant materials, cover with water, and soak overnight.

The next day boil for 1 hour. Strain, and discard the plant material. Add cold water to the liquid to make 2 gallons. Bring to a boil, and add the wool, which has oxidized to a rust color. Turn the heat off, and let the wool remain in the pot overnight. The next day rinse and dry.

## SOURWOOD *Nyssa sylvatica* Marsh.

OTHER NAMES:    Pepperidge, sour gum, tupelo.

PLANT DESCRIPTION:    A tree growing to 100 feet in height with noticeable horizontal limbs. The oval leaves are 2 to 5 inches long, shiny above and downy below. The small greenish-white flowers mature into dark blue fleshy fruits.

114.  Sourwood (*U. S. Department of Agriculture*)

WHERE IT GROWS:    It is widely distributed from New England to Florida, Texas, Oklahoma, and Mexico. It prefers moist areas such as swamps, low, wet woods, and shores of lakes.

PARTS USED:    Leaves, bark.

OTHER COLORS:    Green, tan.

## MORDANT

None required.

## DYE BATH

| | |
|---|---|
| Sourwood leaves | 1 gallon |
| Black walnut roots | 1½ quarts |
| Water | |

Cover the sourwood leaves with water, and seal in a pot. Let the mixture set in a warm place for 3 to 7 days until it ferments.

Layer the black walnut roots and wool in a cooking pot, and then add the sourwood liquid. Boil gently for 2 hours. Rinse and dry.

# CHAPTER 14

# Gray dyes

BEARBERRY *Arctostaphylos uva-ursi* (L.) Spreng.

OTHER NAMES: Arberry, bear's grape, coralillo, hog cranberry, kinnikinnick, mealberry, upland cranberry, uva-ursi.

PLANT DESCRIPTION: A creeping shrub, with stems to 6 inches in height with papery, shredding red bark. The shiny green leaves are 1½ inches long and tapering. The tiny white flowers grow in clusters. The small red fruits are dry and mealy, ¼ to ⅓ inch in diameter.

WHERE IT GROWS: Western United States from the Pacific Northwest and California to New Mexico and Arizona. It prefers dry sunny areas and higher altitudes.

PART USED: Leaves.

### MORDANT

| | |
|---|---|
| Alum | ¾ cup |
| Cream of tartar | ¼ cup |
| Water | 2 gallons |

Dissolve the alum and cream of tartar in the water and bring to a boil. Add the wet wool, and boil gently for 30 minutes. Hang up to dry.

## DYE BATH

Bearberry leaves 2 gallons
Water

Chop the leaves up, cover with water, and soak overnight. The next day boil for 1 hour. Strain and discard the leaves. Add cold water to make 2 gallons. Bring to a boil, and add the dampened, mordanted wool. Boil gently for 45 minutes. Rinse and dry.

115a. (*U. S. Department of Agriculture*)

115. Bearberry (*U. S. Forest Service*)

## BLUEBERRY *Vaccinium* spp.*

### MORDANT

| | |
|---|---|
| Alum | ¼ cup |
| Cream of tartar | ¼ cup |
| Water | 2 gallons |

Dissolve the alum and cream of tartar in the water. Bring to a boil and add the wet wool. Boil gently for 30 minutes. Hang up to dry.

### DYE BATH

| | |
|---|---|
| Blueberries | 2 quarts |
| Water | |

Cover the berries with water and boil for 30 minutes. Strain and discard the pulp. Add cold water to the liquid to make 2 gallons. Bring to a boil, and add the dampened, mordanted wool. Boil gently for 1 hour. Rinse and dry.

## BRAMBLE *Rubus* spp.**

### MORDANT

| | |
|---|---|
| Alum | 1 cup |
| Cream of tartar | ¼ cup |
| Water | 2 gallons |

Dissolve the alum and cream of tartar in the water. Bring to a boil, and add the wet wool. Boil gently for 1 hour. Hang up to dry.

### DYE BATH

| | |
|---|---|
| Bramble fruits, ripe | 1 gallon |
| Salt | 2 tablespoons |
| Water | |

* See Chapter 9 for botanical information.
** See Chapter 13 for botanical information.

Crush the berries, cover with water, and boil for 30 minutes. Strain, and discard the pulp. Add cold water to the liquid to make 2 gallons. Bring to a boil, and add the salt. Stir well, and add the dampened, mordanted wool. Boil gently for 40 minutes. Rinse and dry.

## BUTTERNUT *Juglans cinerea* L.

OTHER NAMES: Filnut, lemonnut, oilnut, white walnut.

PLANT DESCRIPTION: A tree growing to 100 feet in height with gray bark and spreading branches. The leaves, 2 to 5 inches long, are toothed and downy. The fruits, about 3 inches long, grow in bunches of 2 to 5, are sticky and smooth with about 4 ridges where the hull separates into segments.

WHERE IT GROWS: It is found at high elevations at moist sites from Georgia, Alabama, Arkansas, and Mississippi to Kentucky, Tennessee, West Virginia, and Virginia and as far west as North

116. Butternut (*U. S. Forest Service*)

Dakota. This tree was widely used to dye uniforms worn by Confederate troops during the Civil War to a color called butternut.

PART USED:    Green hulls, fresh or dried.

OTHER COLOR:    Brown.

## MORDANT

(For cotton only)
| | |
|---|---|
| Alum | 1 cup |
| Washing soda | ¼ cup |
| Water | 2 gallons |

Dissolve the alum and washing soda in the water, and bring to a boil. Add the wet cotton, and boil gently for 1 hour. Hang up to dry.

## DYE BATH

| | |
|---|---|
| Butternut hulls, green | 3 gallons |
| Water | |

Chop the hulls, cover with water and soak for 30 minutes. Boil for 30 minutes and strain. Discard the hulls and add cold water to the liquid to make 2 gallons. Bring to a boil, and add the dampened, mordanted cotton. Boil gently for 30 minutes. Then transfer to a bath containing:

| | |
|---|---|
| Copperas | 1½ teaspoons |
| Water, boiling | 2 gallons |

Boil gently for 10 minutes. Rinse and dry.

## CHITTIM *Rhamnus purshiana* DC.

OTHER NAMES:    Bitter bark, California coffee, cascara, cascara sagrada, chittern, coffee-berry, coffee-tree, Oregon bearwood, wahoo, Western coffee.

PLANT DESCRIPTION:    A tree growing to 25 feet or more in height with oblong to elliptical toothed leaves 2 to 6 inches long. The small greenish-white flowers occur in umbrella-shaped clusters on short stems. The small black fruits are ¼ inch across.

WHERE IT GROWS:   The species illustrated is a Western plant, found from British Columbia, south to Montana and Northern California. Related species are found in Southeastern states and from North Carolina to Florida. They usually prefer shaded cool areas.

PARTS USED:   Berries, made into an extract, bark.

OTHER COLORS:   Brown, yellow.

## MORDANT

(For cotton only)
| Alum | 2 cups |
| Washing soda | ½ cup |
| Tannic acid | 2 tablespoons |
| Water | |

Dissolve 1 cup of the alum and ¼ cup of the washing soda in 2

117.   Chittim
(*New York
Botanical Garden*)

gallons of water. Add the wet cotton, and bring to a boil. Boil gently for 1 hour. Let the cotton remain in the bath overnight.

The next day bring 2 gallons of water to a boil and add the tannic acid. Remove the cotton from the water that it has been sitting in, squeeze gently, and add to the hot bath containing the tannic acid. Boil gently for 1 hour, stirring frequently. Let the cotton remain in this overnight.

The next day dissolve the remaining cup of alum and ¼ cup of washing soda in 2 gallons of hot water. Remove the cotton from the pot it has been sitting in and rinse. Add the cotton to the bath containing the alum and washing soda, and boil gently for 1 hour, stirring occasionally. Let the cotton remain in the bath overnight.

The next day squeeze the cotton out and hang up to dry.

## DYE BATH

| | |
|---|---|
| Chittim bark | 2 gallons |
| Water | |

Chop the bark, cover with water, and soak overnight. The next day boil for 2 hours and strain. Discard the bark and add cold water to the liquid to make 2 gallons. Bring to a boil, and add the dampened, mordanted cotton. Boil gently for 30 minutes. Transfer to a bath containing:

| | |
|---|---|
| Copperas | 1½ teaspoons |
| Water, boiling | 2 gallons |

Boil gently for 10 minutes. Rinse and dry.

## COUCH GRASS *Agropyron repens* (L.) Beauv.

OTHER NAMES: Blue-joint, devil's grass, dog-grass, false wheat, pond-grass, quitch-grass, Scotch-grass, sea grass, twitch-grass, whickens.

PLANT DESCRIPTION: A perennial growing to 3 feet in height. The flat green blades, 3 to 12 inches long and ⅓ inch wide, are rough above and smooth below. The seed stalk strongly resembles wheat.

118. Couch Grass
(*U. S. Department
of Agriculture*)

WHERE IT GROWS:   New England west to Minnesota, and south
to North Carolina. Prairies, gravelly and sandy shores, fields, roadsides, and waste places.

PART USED:   Roots.

## MORDANT

| | |
|---|---|
| Alum | 1 cup |
| Cream of tartar | ¼ cup |
| Water | 2 gallons |

Dissolve the alum and cream of tartar in the water. Bring to a boil,
and add the wet wool. Boil gently for 1 hour. Hang up to dry.

## DYE BATH

Couch grass roots    1½ gallons
Water

Chop the roots, cover with water, and soak overnight. The next day boil for 1 hour. Strain, and discard the roots. Add cold water to the liquid to make 2 gallons. Bring to a boil, and add the dampened, mordanted wool. Rinse and dry.

## HORSETAIL *Equisetum* spp.

OTHER NAMES:    Bottlebrush, cornfield horsetail, green foxtail rush, horsepipe, horsetail fern, meadow pine, pine grass, pinetop, scouring rush, snake grass.

PLANT DESCRIPTION:    A plant with round, hollow stems, to 3 feet or more in height with whorls of branches at the joints. The joints are grooved and ridged, and pull apart easily. The fruiting body is a conelike structure.

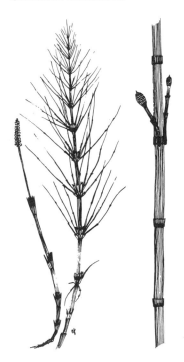

119.  Horsetail (*U. S. Department of Agriculture*)

WHERE IT GROWS: From Alaska southward to all parts of the United States. It is found in all kinds of sites from rich forests to shores, marshes, and swamps.

PART USED: Stalks.

## MORDANT

| | |
|---|---|
| Alum | 1 cup |
| Cream of tartar | ¼ cup |
| Water | 2 gallons |

Dissolve the alum and cream of tartar in the water, and bring to a boil. Add the wet wool and boil gently for 30 minutes. Hang up to dry.

## DYE BATH

| | |
|---|---|
| Horsetail stalks | 2 quarts |
| Water | |

Chop the stalks, cover with water, and soak overnight. The next day boil for 1 hour. Strain and discard the stalks. Add cold water to the liquid to make 2 gallons. Bring to a boil, and add the dampened, mordanted wool. Boil for 30 minutes. Rinse and dry.

## MAPLE *Acer* spp.

PLANT DESCRIPTION: These plants vary from large bushes to trees to 100 feet in height. The toothed leaves range from light to dark green with 3 to 5 lobes. The flowers are greenish yellow with 5 petals. The seeds are winged nuts.

WHERE IT GROWS: The various maples are widely distributed throughout Eastern Canada, New England, and the Northeastern states west to Iowa, Michigan, and Wisconsin, and south to Kentucky, Tennessee, and Georgia. They are found under many different growing conditions but seem to prefer cool and moist areas.

PART USED: Bark.

OTHER COLOR: Brown.

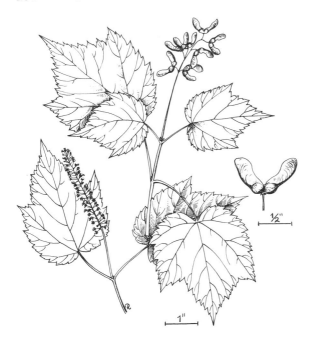

120. Maple (*U. S. Forest Service*)

## MORDANT

(For cotton only)

| | |
|---|---|
| Alum | 2 cups |
| Washing soda | ½ cup |
| Tannic acid | 2 tablespoons |
| Water | |

Dissolve 1 cup of the alum and ¼ cup of the washing soda in 2 gallons of water. Add the wet cotton, and bring to a boil. Boil gently for 1 hour. Let the cotton cool in the bath overnight.

The next day bring 2 gallons of water to a boil and add the tannic acid. Remove the cotton from the water that it has been sitting in, squeeze gently, and add to the hot bath containing the tannic acid. Boil gently for 1 hour, stirring frequently. Let the cotton remain in the bath overnight.

The next day dissolve the remaining cup of alum and ¼ cup of washing soda in 2 gallons of hot water. Remove the cotton from the bath that it has been sitting in and rinse. Add the cotton to the bath containing the alum and washing soda, and boil gently for 1 hour, stirring frequently. Let the cotton remain in the bath overnight.

The next day squeeze the cotton out and hang up to dry.

## DYE BATH

Maple bark    2 gallons
Water

Chop the bark, cover with water, and soak overnight. The next day boil for 1½ hours. Strain, and discard the bark. Add cold water to the liquid to make 2 gallons. Bring to a boil, and add the dampened, mordanted cotton. Boil gently for 45 minutes. Transfer to a bath containing:

Potassium dichromate    1½ teaspoons
Vinegar    2 gallons
Water, boiling    ⅓ cup

Boil gently for 10 minutes. Rinse and dry.


## RHODODENDRON *Rhododendron* spp.

OTHER NAME:  Rose bay.

PLANT DESCRIPTION:  A wide range of shrubs growing from 6 to 35 feet in height. The most familiar ones are evergreen with glossy, thick leaves; a few are deciduous and drop their leaves. The flowers grow in bunches on the ends of the branches and resemble umbrellas and come in almost all colors. Many species exist all over the world, and many ornamentals have been introduced into the United States.

WHERE IT GROWS:  Although they are most common east of the Mississippi, native species are found in California, Oregon, and Washington. Garden specimens can be found in many states. They are shade and moisture lovers and are found along streams in heavy hardwood forests and sometimes in dry sand hills.

PART USED:  Leaves.


## MORDANT

None required.

121.  Rhododendron (*U. S. Forest Service*)

## DYE BATH

| | |
|---|---|
| Rhododendron leaves | 2 gallons |
| Copperas | ¼ cup |
| Water | |

Chop the leaves, cover with water, and soak overnight. The next day boil for 2 hours. Strain, and discard the leaves. Add cold water to the liquid to make 2 gallons. Bring to a boil and add the copperas. Stir well, and add the wet wool. Boil gently for 30 minutes. Rinse and dry.

## SUMAC *Rhus glabra* L.,* *Rhus copallina* L.

### MORDANT

For wool or cotton, none required.

### DYE BATH

| | |
|---|---|
| Sumac berries, ripe | 3 gallons |
| Copperas | 1 tablespoon |
| Water | |

Crush the berries, cover with water, and soak for 1 hour. Boil for 30 minutes, and strain. Discard the berries and add cold water to the liquid to make 2 gallons. Bring to a boil, and add the copperas. Stir well, and add the wet, unmordanted material. Boil gently for 30 minutes. Transfer to a bath containing:

| | |
|---|---|
| Copperas | 1 ½ teaspoons |
| Water, boiling | 2 gallons |

Boil gently for 10 minutes. Rinse and dry.

## WHITE SASSAFRAS *Sassafras albidum* (Nutal) Nees.**

### MORDANT

*METHOD 1*

| | |
|---|---|
| (For wool) | |
| Potassium dichromate | 2 tablespoons |
| Water | 2 gallons |

Bring the water to a boil, and add the potassium dichromate. Stir

* See Chapter 13 for botanical information.
** See Chapter 12 for botanical information.

well and add the wet wool. Boil gently for 1 hour. Let the wool cool in the water, and then hang up to dry.

(For cotton only)
| | |
|---|---|
| Alum | 2 cups |
| Washing soda | ½ cup |
| Tannic acid | 2 tablespoons |
| Water | |

Dissolve 1 cup of the alum and ¼ cup of the washing soda in 2 gallons of water. Add the wet cotton, and bring to a boil. Boil gently for 1 hour. Let the cotton cool in the bath overnight.

The next day bring 2 gallons of water to a boil and add the tannic acid. Remove the cotton from the water that it has been sitting in, squeeze gently, and add to the hot water containing the tannic acid. Boil gently for 1 hour, stirring frequently. Let the cotton remain in the bath overnight.

The next day dissolve the remaining cup of alum and ¼ cup of washing soda in 2 gallons of hot water. Remove the cotton from the pot that it has been sitting in and rinse. Add the cotton to the bath containing the alum and washing soda, and boil gently for 1 hour, stirring occasionally. Let the cotton remain in the bath overnight.

The next day squeeze the cotton out and hang up to dry.


## DYE BATH

| | |
|---|---|
| Sassafras root bark | 1 quart |
| Water | |

Chop the root bark, cover with water, and soak overnight. The next day boil for 30 minutes. Strain and discard the root bark. Add cold water to the liquid to make 2 gallons. Bring to a boil and add the dampened, mordanted wool or cotton. Boil gently for 40 minutes. Transfer to a bath containing:

| | |
|---|---|
| Copperas | 1½ teaspoons |
| Water, boiling | 2 gallons |

Boil gently for 10 minutes. Rinse and dry.

## MORDANT

| | |
|---|---|
| Alum | ¾ cup |
| Cream of tartar | ¼ cup |
| Water | 2 gallons |

Bring the water to a boil, and add the alum and cream of tartar. Stir well and add the wet wool. Boil gently for 1 hour. Let the wool cool in the water, and then hang up to dry.

## DYE BATH

| | |
|---|---|
| Sassafras root bark | 1 quart |
| Water | |

Chop the root bark, cover with water, and soak overnight. The next day boil for 30 minutes. Strain and discard the root bark. Add cold water to the liquid to make 2 gallons. Bring to a boil and add the dampened, mordanted wool. Boil gently for 40 minutes. Transfer to a bath containing:

| | |
|---|---|
| Potassium dichromate | 1½ teaspoons |
| Water, boiling | 2 gallons |

Boil gently for 10 minutes. Rinse and dry.

## YARROW *Achillea millefolium* L.

OTHER NAMES: Bloodwort, carpenter's grass, dog daisy, green arrow, milfoil, nosebleed, old man's pepper, sanguinary, soldier's woundwort, thousand leaf.

PLANT DESCRIPTION: A graceful, aromatic growing to 3 feet in height. Foliage is finely cut, the leaves lack stalks. The white to purple flowers are clustered densely at the top of the plant.

WHERE IT GROWS:    It is found throughout Canada and the United States in old pastures, abandoned fields, roadsides, and openings in forests.

PARTS USED:    Flowers, leaves.

OTHER COLOR:    Green.

122.  Yarrow (*Colorado State University, from* WEEDS OF COLORADO)

## MORDANT

None required.

## DYE BATH

| | |
|---|---|
| Yarrow flowers and leaves | 2 gallons |
| Copperas | 2 teaspoons |
| Water | |

Chop the flowers and leaves, and cover with water. Boil for 30 minutes. Strain and discard the plant material. Add cold water to the liquid to make 2 gallons. Bring to a boil and add the copperas. Stir well and add the wet, unmordanted wool. Boil gently for 40 minutes. Rinse and dry.

# Bibliography

ADROSKO, RITA J. *Natural Dyes in the United States.* Washington, D.C., Smithsonian Institution Press. 1968.

BANCROFT, EDWARD, M.D. *Experimental Researches Concerning the Philosophy of Permanent Colors.* 2 vols. Philadelphia. 1814.

BEMISS, ELIJAH. *The Dyers Companion.* New London and New York, Everet Duyckinck. 1806 and 1815.

BENSON, ADOLF B. (ed.). *Peter Kalm's Travels in North America.* 2 vols. New York, Wilson-Erikson, Inc. 1937.

*The Best System of Dyeing.* Bennington, Vermont. 1811.

BIRCH, THOMAS. *History of the Royal Society of London.* 4 vols. London. 1756–57.

BISHOP, J. LEANDER. *A History of American Manufacturers from 1608 to 1860.* 3 vols. Philadelphia, Edward Young and Co. 1866.

BOLTON, EILEEN M. *Lichens for Vegetable Dyeing.* Newton Centre, Mass., Charles T. Branford Co. 1960.

BRONSON, J. and R. *The Domestic Manufacturers Assistant, and Family Directory, in the Arts of Weaving and Dyeing.* Utica, N.Y. 1817.

Bureau of American Ethnology. Annual report of 1881–82, pp. 371–97. Washington, D.C. Government Printing Office. 1884.

Bureau of American Ethnology. 30th annual report, 1908–9, pp. 31–116. Washington, D.C. Government Printing Office. 1915.

CATESBY, MARK. *The Natural History of Carolina, Florida, and the Bahama Islands.* 2 vols., 3rd ed. London, Benjamin White. 1771.

CONLEY, EMMA. *Vegetable Dyeing.* Penland, N.C., Penland School of Crafts. (n.d.)

COOPER, THOMAS. *A Practical Treatise on Dyeing, and Callicoe Printing.* Philadelphia, Thomas Dobson. 1815.

CROAKES, SIR WILLIAM. *A Practical Handbook of Dyeing and Calico-Printing.* London, Longmans, Green and Co. 1874.

DAVIDSON, MARY FRANCES. *The Dye-Pot.* Middlesboro, Kentucky, Shuttlecraft Shop. 1959.

ELLIS, ASA, JR. *The Country Dyer's Assistant.* Brookfield, Mass. 1798.

FURRY, MARGARET S., and BESS M. VIEMONT. *Home Dyeing with Natural Dyes.* Washington, D.C. U.S.D.A., Misc. publication no. 230. 1935.

GERARD, JOHN. *The Herbal.* London. 1597.

GILROY, CLINTON G. *A Practical Treatise on Dyeing and Calico-Printing.* 2nd ed., rev. New York, Harper and Bros. 1846.

GRABILL, EPHRAIM. *The Art of Dyeing All Sorts of Colours, Containing 36 Secrets. For the Use of Families.* 2nd ed. (Hanover, Pa. ?), 1846.

HAIGH, JAMES. *The Dier's Assistant in the Art of Dying Wool and Woolen Goods* . . . 1st Amer. ed. Philadelphia, 1810. 2nd Amer. ed. Poughkeepsie, N.Y., Paraclete Potter. 1813.

HARDT, PETER. *The Family Dyer.* (English and German) York, Pa. 1819.

HASERIC, E. C. *The Secrets of the Art of Dyeing.* Cambridge, Mass. 1869.

HEDRICK, U. P. (ed.). *Sturtevant's Notes on Edible Plants.* New York Department of Agriculture, 27th annual report, vol. 2, Part II. Albany, N.Y., J. B. Lyons Company, State Printers. 1919.

HEUSSER, ALBERT HENRY (ed.). *The History of the Silk Dyeing Industry in the United States.* Paterson, N.J., published for the Silk Dyers Association of America. 1937.

HURRY, JAMIESON B. *The Woad Plant and Its Dye.* London, Oxford University Press. 1930.

JEFFERSON, THOMAS. *Thomas Jefferson's Garden Book.* Edwin Morris Betts (ed.), Amer. Philos. Soc. Mem., vol. 22. Philadelphia. 1944.

KALM, PETER. *Travels into North America.* 2nd ed. 2 vols. London, John Reinhold Forster, translator. 1772.

KIERSTEAD, SALLIE PEASE. *Natural Dyes.* Boston, Humphries. 1950.

KNECHT, RAWSON. *A Manual of Dyeing.* 2nd ed. 2 vols. London, Charles Griffin and Co. 1910.

KOK, ANNETTE. *A Short History of the Orchil Dyes.* The Lichenologist. Part 2, pp. 248–72, London, British Lichen Society. 1968.

KROCHMAL, ARNOLD, et al. *A Guide to Medicinal Plants of Appalachia.* Agricultural Handbook 400. Washington, D.C., U.S.D.A. 1971.

KROCHMAL, ARNOLD, and CONNIE KROCHMAL. *Guide to Medicinal Plants of the United States*. New York, Quadrangle Books. 1973.

KROCHMAL, ARNOLD, and SHERMAN PAUR. *Canaigre—A Desert Source of Tannin*. Economic Botany, 1951, 5(4): 367–77.

KROCHMAL, ARNOLD, SHERMAN PAUR, and P. DUISBERG. *Useful Native Plants in the American Southwestern Deserts*. Economic Botany, 1954, 8(1): 332–37.

LAWRIE, L. G. *A Bibliography of Dyeing and Textile Printing*. London, Chapman and Hall, Ltd. 1949.

LEECHMAN, DOUGLAS. *Vegetable Dyes from North American Plants*. St. Paul, The Webb Pub. Co. 1945.

LEGGETT, WILLIAM FERGUSEN. *Ancient and Medieval Dyes*. Brooklyn, N.Y. Chemical Publishing Co., Inc. 1944.

LYNDE, J. *The Domestic Dyer*. New York (State). 1831.

MACKENZIE, COLIN. *Mackenzie's Five Thousand Recipts in All the Useful and Domestic Arts*. Philadelphia. 1831.

MAGNESS, J. R., G. M. MARKLE, and C. C. COMPTON. *Food and Feed Crops of the United States*. New Jersey Agricultural Experiment Station, Bulletin 828, New Brunswick, N.J. 1971.

MAIRET, ETHEL M. *Vegetable Dyes, Being a Book of Recipes and Other Information Useful to the Dyer*. London, Faber and Faber, Ltd. 1948.

MATTHEWS, WASHINGTON. *Navajo Dye Stuffs*. pp. 613–15. Smithsonian Institution annual report, Washington, D.C. 1893.

MOLONY, CORNELIUS. *The Modern Wool Dyer Containing the Most Approved Methods as Practiced in the First Clothing Establishments in Great Britain*. Lowell, Mass. 1834.

———. *The Practical Dyer*. Boston. 1833.

O'NEILL, CHARLES. *A Dictionary of Dyeing and Calico Printing*. Philadelphia, Henry Carey Baird. 1869.

PINCKNEY, ELISE (ed.). *The Letterbook of Eliza Lucas Pinckney, 1739–1762*. Chapel Hill, N.C., University of North Carolina Press. 1972.

*Purple Dyeing, Ancient and Modern*. Smithsonian Institution annual report. pp. 385–403. Washington, D.C. 1864.

RAUCH, JOHN. *John Rauch's Receipts on Dyeing*. New York, Joseph I. Badger & Co. 1815.

RAVENEL, HARRIOT. *Eliza Pinckney*. New York, Scribner's. 1909.

SCHETKY, ETHEL JANE MCD. (ed.). *Dye Plants and Dyeing—a Handbook,* Plants and Gardens, 20(3), Brooklyn, N.Y., Brooklyn Botanic Garden. 1964.

SHARRER, G. TERRY. *Indigo in Carolina, 1671–1796.* Technology and Culture, 12(3), July 1971, pp. 94–103. The Society for the History of Technology.

———. *The Indigo Bonanza in South Carolina, 1740–90.* The South Carolina Historical Magazine, 72(2), April 1971, pp. 448–55. South Carolina Historical Society, Charleston, S.C.

SHELDON, WILLIAM. *Application of Chestnut Wood to the Arts of Tanning and Dyeing. Philosophical Magazine and Journal,* vol. 54, July–December 1819, pp. 148–50. London, Edinburgh, and Dublin.

SHELTON, FERNE. *Pioneer Comforts and Kitchen Remedies.* High Point, N.C., Hutchcraft. 1965.

SMITH, D. *The Dyer's Instructor.* Philadelphia. 1853, 1857, 1866.

SUDWORT, GEORGE B., and CLAYTON, D. MELL. *Fustic Wood; Its Substitutes and Adulterants.* Forest Service Circular 184. U.S.D.A., Washington, D.C.

TOMLINSON, CHARLES, (ed.). *Cyclopaedia of Useful Arts.* 2 vols. London. 1854.

TUCKER, WILLIAM. *The Family Dyer and Scourer.* 4th London ed. Philadelphia, E. L. Carey and A. Hart. Ca. 1830.

U. S. Tariff Commission. *The Dyestuff Situation in the Textile Industries.* Tariff Information Series, no. 2. Washington, D.C. 1918.

U. S. Tariff Commission. *Census of Dyes and Coal-tar Chemicals.* Tariff Information Series, no. 6. Washington, D.C. 1918.

VINER, WILMER STONE, and H. E. VINER. *The Katherine Pettit Book of Vegetable Dyes.* Saluda, N.C., The Excelsior Printers. 1946.

WAITE, DANIEL, & CO. *The New American Dier.* Brookfield, Mass. 1815.

WHERRY, JOSEPH H. *The Totem Pole Indians.* New York, Wilfred Funk, Inc. 1964.

# Index

# INDEX